Writing Matters

Writing Matters

Writing skills and strategies
for students of English

*Kristine Brown and
Susan Hood*

CAMBRIDGE
UNIVERSITY PRESS

PUBLISHED BY THE PRESS SYNDICATE OF THE UNIVERSITY OF CAMBRIDGE
The Pitt Building, Trumpington Street, Cambridge, United Kingdom

CAMBRIDGE UNIVERSITY PRESS
The Edinburgh Building, Cambridge CB2 2RU, UK
40 West 20th Street, New York, NY 10011–4211, USA
477 Williamstown Road, Port Melbourne, VIC 3207, Australia
Ruiz de Alarcón 13, 28014 Madrid, Spain
Dock House, The Waterfront, Cape Town 8001, South Africa

http://www.cambridge.org

First published 1989
Eleventh printing 2002

Printed in the United Kingdom at the University Press, Cambridge

ISBN 0 521 34895 1

Contents

Thanks

The authors would like to thank their colleagues in New South Wales, Victoria and the ACT for their comments and suggestions during the writing of this book. We would also like to thank the students who took part in the trialling of the material.

We are very grateful to Annemarie Young, Alison Silver and Adrian du Plessis for their encouragement and advice, to Sue Wright and Nicky Solomon for their great help in the preparation of the manuscript, and to our families and Dr Swami for their patience and support.

To the student

About the book

This book is to help you develop your writing ability in English, so that you feel more confident about the writing you need to do in everyday life. The exercises give you the opportunity to practise this day-to-day sort of writing (e.g. job applications, personal letters, notes and messages). They give you help with the aspects of writing you might find difficult (e.g. the organization of ideas, choosing the right word, linking ideas, paragraphing, spelling, punctuation). Units 4 and 5 give you special help with spelling and punctuation.

The exercises show you that *how* you write depends on:
– *who* you are writing to (your *reader*)
– *why* you are writing (your *purpose*)
– *what* you are writing *about* (your *content*)
– *where* and *when* you are writing (the *situation*).
So you are not always asked to write in a formally correct way.

The exercises emphasize that writing is a *process* which always requires some preparation, drafting and revising. You are not asked to 'get everything right' the first time. You get special help with the process of writing in Units 1, 2 and 3.

Units 6–13 help you with writing that you often need or want to do. Units 14–16 give you ideas for personal, creative and fun writing.

In Units 6–16, the exercises at the beginning of each unit ask you to practise only one or two aspects of writing at a time (e.g. punctuation, layout). The exercises towards the end of these units are more open-ended, and ask you to practise more features of writing. In these later exercises there is the opportunity to choose situations and tasks that are *personally* relevant to you.

There is a lot of opportunity to develop and practise your reading and speaking skills in this book. You are often asked to look at other people's writing and to discuss it. This is a good way of improving your own writing.

Using the book

If you are working alone, it is *especially* important that you read this part carefully. It will help you get the most benefit from the book.

The book is in two parts, with each part divided into two sub-sections. It is best to begin with Part 1, *The writing process*, Units 1, 2 and 3. These are important to *all* other units.

You should then begin the *Writing sub-skills*, *Spelling* and *Punctuation*, Units 4 and 5. Do not try to complete either of these units in one session. In Unit 4,

Spelling, do only one part at a time (e.g. identifying spelling errors, spelling unfamiliar words). In Unit 5, *Punctuation*, do only two or three items of punctuation at a time (e.g. capital letters, full stops).

While working on these, you should begin on Part 2, *Context units*. Choose whichever units you want to do. It doesn't matter in which order you do them, except that you should do Unit 10, *Formal letters*, before Units 11–13.

In every unit, it is essential to work through the Introduction. In each Context unit, the Introduction gives you a model of writing and a number of important points to study. If you are working alone, it is very important that you think about (and perhaps write down the answers to) any questions you are asked to discuss here.

After this, choose exercises which match your needs and interests. Wherever an exercise gives you a choice, think about a reader, a purpose, content and a situation which are personally relevant to you. (Think of a friend you really want to write a letter to, think of an issue you have a strong opinion on, include details from your personal life on a postcard.)

Wherever possible, *do* something with your writing (send your letter, submit your opinion to the editor of your class or school magazine, send your postcard). If you do not have a class or school magazine, you could help to organize one!

In most units, there are a few exercises which ask you to discuss or work with other students. If you are working alone, it is best to write down your thoughts in these exercises.

It is a good idea to collect examples of writing, and to use these as extra models for your own writing.

There are answers at the back of the book for exercises where there are only one or two answers possible, or where a model answer seems necessary.

To the teacher

About the book

The aim of this book is to help students at the low intermediate to intermediate level to develop their writing ability in English and to give them the confidence to use this ability in everyday life. Students at this level usually want to and need to write independently, but often avoid it or handle it less proficiently than they do speaking, listening or reading.

The reasons for this are many and varied, but in this book we aim to break down four major barriers to student confidence. The first is that because writing is a more permanent record of one's language proficiency than is speaking, the demand for unrehearsed writing is more threatening to the learner. The second is that learners often feel that they do not have the necessary knowledge and experience of language that writing demands. The third barrier is the view, often reinforced in classroom texts, that writing must be correct, in a formal sense, irrespective of context. The fourth is the related view that such formal correctness must be achieved first time round in a one-off writing attempt.

This book aims to address directly each of these issues. Firstly, it provides non-threatening guided opportunities to practise (or rehearse) the very sort of writing tasks that are required in real life. Secondly, it provides guidance and practice in the aspects of language and form so important to effective writing. So, you find models of different types of texts with explanations and discussion points. You find exercises which deal, for example, with organization and ordering of ideas, paragraphing, linking ideas, appropriate word choice, economy of phrasing, layout, spelling and punctuation. (Particular focus on these last two is provided in Units 4 and 5.) Thirdly, the book emphasizes that the demands of writing vary considerably depending on the proposed reader, the purpose, the content and the writing situation. Students are urged to think about the relationship between these four determinant factors and the features of written language above. For example, there are exercises on appropriate wording to achieve results in letters of protest or complaint, exercises on economic use of words to keep down cost in advertisements, and so on. Lastly, it reflects throughout that writing is a process which always, but to varying extents and in varying ways, requires preparation, drafting and revising. The exercises help students to be more aware of this process and thereby to improve the effectiveness of their writing. (Particular focus on this is provided in Units 1, 2 and 3.)

The book does not aim to teach items of vocabulary or grammar, except where such items seem to be specific enough to the writing context and important enough to the successful completion of the tasks being set to warrant special guidance and practice. There are many textbooks which do teach these things and students and teachers may want to refer to these as they use this book. The exercises in this book will however provide a realistic and relevant context within which students can practise any newly acquired items of grammar and vocabulary.

Although written primarily for adult students for whom English is a Second Language, we also see this book as being useful for adult native speakers of English who wish to improve their everyday writing, and for secondary school students.

The writing contexts in Part 2 were chosen on the basis of their appropriateness for adult students at this level in terms of interest and need. Writing extracts used as models or within exercises were chosen on the same basis and also because of their appropriateness in terms of language complexity.

Although the emphasis is on functional writing, there is also opportunity provided for non-functional writing. Units 14, 15 and 16 consist of exercises directed at more creative and imaginative writing.

The exercises vary somewhat in level of complexity to cater for all students in the target group. As well, there is flexibility within many exercises to provide for response at a variety of levels. In the Context units (6–16), there is a progression from exercises which focus on specific and therefore more manageable aspects of writing to those which are more open-ended and uncontrolled. Along with this progression goes the increased opportunity for individual response.

Opportunity for developing reading skills exists with the provision of writing models and with exercises where students must respond in writing to something they have read. In addition, there is opportunity for discussion. In Units 6–16, students are asked to talk about their own experiences and needs, and to study and discuss the writing models presented.

Using the book

The book is arranged in two parts, with each part divided into two sub-sections. We feel it is best to begin with Part 1, *The writing process*, Units 1, 2, 3, and to work through them systematically, as these units are relevant to all subsequent units. The exercises in them, though unavoidably dealing with some of the contexts to follow, demand as little as possible in the way of exact knowledge and experience of those contexts.

The *Writing sub-skills* units – Unit 4, *Spelling* and Unit 5, *Punctuation* – are best worked through next, concurrently with a context unit from Part 2. You are advised not to attempt to cover all of Unit 4 or Unit 5 in a single lesson. In Unit 4, *Spelling* it would be best to take one part per lesson (e.g. identifying spelling errors, spelling unfamiliar words), so taking at the least four lessons to complete it. In Unit 5, *Punctuation* it would be best to do two or three items of punctuation per lesson, so taking twelve or thirteen lessons to finish.

While doing Units 4 and 5, you should begin on Part 2, the *Context units*. They are arranged roughly in order of complexity and typical length of texts, but except for Unit 10, *Formal letters*, which is best done before Units 11–13, it does not matter in which order you do them. That will depend more on your students' needs and interests and on other language work you are doing.

In each unit there is an Introduction which gives a background and a purpose to the exercises in the unit. Once a unit is selected it is vital to take students through this Introduction. After this, your choice of exercises will, again, depend on student need and interest. In exercises where choice is given it is important to encourage students to think of readers and purposes, content and situations personally relevant to them. Wherever possible they should be encouraged to publish their writing (send a personal letter or postcard to a friend, send off a job application, submit a letter to the editor of the local paper or to the editor of the class magazine). The production of a class or school magazine, mentioned in many parts of the book as a venue for publication, is particularly relevant in Units 12, 13, 15 and 16 as a means of providing an interested audience and a real purpose for writing.

In all Context units it would be a good idea to encourage students to bring in examples of writing and to use these as further models for study and discussion.

Answers are provided at the back of the book where there are a limited number of answers possible or where the provision of a model answer seems necessary.

Part 1: Core units

THE WRITING PROCESS

Introduction

The next three units are very important. They describe the three main stages of the writing process. For ease of discussion, we present these three stages like this:

but in practice the process is often more like this:

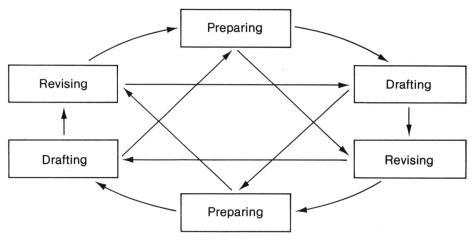

The writing process depends on:
- *who* you are writing to or for (*reader*)
- *why* you are writing (*purpose*)
- *what* you are writing about (*content*)
- *where* you are, *how much time* you have, *how* you feel, etc. (*situation*).
    There is no *one* way to write. The ideas in the next three units are only suggestions. Try them all. Some you may find useful in one type of writing. Some you may find useful every time you write.
    Whatever you do, you will benefit from lots of practice. So *write often* – even if it's only for a short time and even if it's only for yourself.

Many of the exercises which follow continue through the three units, so keep all your writing until the end of Unit 3, Revising.

1 Preparing to write

Introduction

Most writing requires some preparation. How long you spend on this preparation, and what you do, largely depends on your *reader*, your *purpose*, the *content* and the writing *situation*. For example, a quick message to a friend requires different preparation from a letter to a company applying for a job.

The ideas below will be useful to you in preparing to write.

Remember: Keep all the writing you do in these exercises for use in the next two units.

Ideas

BRAINSTORMING

This means you 'storm' or search your brain for ideas.
– Write them down very quickly. They don't have to be in English.
– Don't worry about how useful they will be.
– Don't worry about neatness and correctness.
e.g. Brainstorming in preparation for a job application letter:

Assistant Chef – Advertiser Sat 11th July
Asian cooking is my specialty
2 years experience in America
Prefer part-time work but f/t is ok
Close to home
Don't mind split shifts
3 year certificate course

Exercise 1

Choose an item that interests you from those below. You are going to write something about it for a student magazine (a letter to the editor, an article, a story). Prepare by brainstorming.

(Keep the notes you make for use in exercise 1, Unit 2, *Drafting*.)

Are women the stronger sex?

IN BRIEF

Marriage less popular

DON LANE, talking about his one-year-old son, PJ: "I worry that I'll be 72 when he's 20. It's a big gap. But if I feel as young then as I do now there won't be any problems."

HANG THEM

SOME say hanging criminals makes us as bad as they are. This is not so.

It is done with the minimum of pain and the victims know why they are being hanged.

SPEED WRITING

This is a warm-up activity to get you writing freely.
— Give yourself a time limit (say two minutes).
— Write as much as you possibly can on a topic.
— Write whatever comes into your head. It doesn't matter if it doesn't all make
  sense.
— Keep writing until the time is up.
— Don't worry about neatness and correctness.
e.g. Speed writing in preparation for a letter to a teacher about a child's problems at school:

> P. seems to be very unhappy this year — don't
> really know what the cause is — but I feel I have to
> find out — maybe other students in the class — perhaps
> the teacher — seems to be able to cope OK with the work
> — brings his homework home and doesn't seem to
> mind doing it. He has mentioned another boy
> ...

Exercise 2

Choose from one of the following topics and write a letter to the editor of your
class magazine.
work   children   television
Prepare by doing two minutes speed writing.
  (Keep your writing for exercise 4, Unit 2, *Drafting*.)

ASKING YOURSELF 'WH' QUESTIONS

This idea is useful for longer pieces of writing.
— Write down some questions about the topic.
  who . . . ? what . . . ? where . . . ? when . . . ? why . . . ? how . . . ?
— Think of as many questions as you can.
e.g. 'Wh' questions in preparation for a letter to the Council about the bad
condition of the roads:

> *What is the problem?*
> *Who is being affected by it?*
> *Where is the problem worst?*
> *Why is it so bad here?*
> *When is the Council going to do something?*

Exercise 3

Imagine you are planning to move to another city. You need to have accommodation arranged before you move. Prepare a letter to send to some real estate agents in your new city, telling them what you are looking for. Make up a list of 'wh' questions to remind yourself of what you need to mention in your letter.
e.g. 'When do I need the accommodation?'
(Keep your questions for exercise 3, Unit 2, *Drafting*.)

GETTING YOUR IDEAS INTO ORDER

This is something you could do after brainstorming, speed writing, or 'wh' questions.
– Look through your notes.
– Use numbers or arrows to put them in the order you want to mention them in writing.
e.g. Ordering notes in preparation for a job application letter:

Assistant Chef – Advertiser Sat 11th July
③ Asian cooking is my specialty
② 2 years experience in America
④ Prefer part-time work but f/t is ok
⑥ Close to home
⑤ Don't mind split shifts
① 3 year certificate course

Exercise 4

Below are some notes a writer made in preparing to write a letter of complaint to the Council about the lack of playgrounds in the area. Rewrite the notes in the order you would mention them.

nowhere for children to play
heavy traffic → accidents
most play in streets
worry for parents
need grassy areas – concrete surfaces mean broken bones
somewhere for parents to watch children play
need some playground equipment

Exercise 5

Use some of the notes you made in one of the previous exercises (brainstorming, speed writing, 'wh' questions). Use numbers or arrows to put the notes in the order you want to mention them.

USING MODELS

Models or examples can help you with what to write and how to write it.
– Look for models of the kind of writing you want to do.
– Keep a file of these so you will have them when you need them.
– Think about the content (the information included, the questions asked, the ideas mentioned).
– Look closely at the language used. Underline or make notes of any useful expressions.
– Look closely at the organization of ideas.
The model on the left was useful in writing the advertisement on the right.

```
BABYSITTER required to
mind 8-year-old boy
before and after
school, 3 days/wk.
Preferably with other
school-aged children.
Lewisham area.
Phone Jim after 6pm.
71 3029.
```

Tutor required to help with English, after 5pm, 2 nights/ wk. Preferably in my home. Summer Hill area. Phone Ming after 4.30 p.m.   798·2014

Exercise 6

Imagine you want to sell a refrigerator. Look carefully at the advertisements below.
– Take note of any useful words or abbreviations.
– Discuss with other students the kind of information included, and the order in which it is mentioned.

FOR SALE

CANE CHAIRS (2) one large $35. 1 small $10. 70 3211.

PHILIP TV 63cm color in good condition $350. Lounge 8 seater as new $550. 708 1217.

PHILIPS refrigerator, good working condition, $100.   74 2091.

LARGE green lounge, excellent condition, $50. Garden seats and large pots. 78 8515.

SEWING MACHINE Brother industrial plain sewer, excellent condition, very little use, suit outdoor worker or factory $650. 759 9022 after 6 pm.

SKI BOOTS, ladies' 6½, white & black, men's size 12 in navy, weinmann wind ups, $80 each or best offer. Ladies' stocks included.   71 6801.

Exercise 7

Read the following letter to the editor carefully.

– Write down the three phrases that are used to introduce and to link the writer's three arguments against the death penalty.
– Write down any other useful words or expressions.

SIR, Ms M. Squires of Coogee (24/6/88) writes that hanging criminals is the only way we can stop others from committing serious crimes. I strongly disagree.

In the first place, there is absolutely no evidence to support her claim. What's more, if we as a society murder those who commit murder, we are no better than murderers ourselves.

Violence is no answer to violence. And then there is the question of whether we can ever be 100% sure of a person's guilt. What should happen if an innocent person were hanged? No, Ms Squires, the death penalty is not the answer. What we need instead is a more caring society.

MRS K. HAVEL
Richmond

MARKING POINTS TO MENTION IN REPLY

If you are replying to a letter or advertisement:

– Reread that letter or advertisement.
– Underline parts that you want to mention in reply.
– Keep the letter or advertisement handy when you are writing as a reminder of things to mention.

e.g.

Salesperson

We are seeking a <u>mature</u> person with <u>experience</u> in sales. Some <u>experience with selling power tools</u> would be an advantage, and applicants should hold a current <u>driver's licence</u> and be available for some <u>weekend work</u>.

Salary is negotiable. A company vehicle will be provided. Applications should be directed in writing to:

<u>Mr Alf Singer</u>
<u>Personnel Manager</u>
<u>ANDERSON and LEECH POWER</u>
<u>TOOLS PTY LTD</u>
<u>P.O. Box 635</u>
<u>Port Adelaide 5015</u>

Exercise 8

Van received this letter from some friends overseas. Note the parts he might mention in reply.

Dear Van,
Just a short note to let you know that we have a house now —
690 Wayville Rd
Alexandria, Va.
22307
Just 15 minutes to work by car. Speaking of work, how's your job? Last time you wrote you had only just begun working for a firm in Waterloo. Are you still there?
I haven't heard much news from home lately. What are all the family up to? Write and let me know the important things like who's winning the football and what the weather's been like!
Bye for now
Mary (and Steve)

Additional exercises

Exercise 9

Think of someone you would like to write to, someone you haven't written to for a long time.
- Quickly jot down as many things as you can think of that have happened to you over the last 6 months.
- Group together those events that seem to belong together.
- Decide which you will mention first and a rough order for the rest of your news.

(Keep your notes for exercise 5, Unit 2, *Drafting*.)

Exercise 10

Choose one of the ideas described in this unit to prepare for the following:

a) A note to someone who is minding your house, telling them where everything is.
b) A letter to your landlady asking for some repairs to be done.
c) An advertisement to sell some furniture you no longer want.
d) A story about your childhood.

(Keep your notes for exercise 6, Unit 2, *Drafting*.)

Exercise 11

Think of something you personally need to write at the moment. Prepare for your writing in one of the ways suggested in this unit. (Keep your notes for exercise 7, Unit 2, *Drafting*.)

2 **Drafting**

Introduction

The drafting stage is where you really begin writing. The most important thing here is to get words onto paper. It is not the time to worry about spelling, grammar, punctuation or the best wording.

Look at our first draft of what you have just read. Very messy and very different from the final product, isn't it?

In this unit, we will { concentrate / focus on

the first draft only. This is _where_ the part (?)

you { really / actually begin writing, after some

preparation (notes, brainstorming - - - - -).

? { The most important thing at this

stage is to get words onto the

paper. { It / This is not the time to

worry about things like grammar,

spelling, punctuation etc. - - - -

In this unit we will concentrate on writing a first draft. There is no *one* way to do this. Some people make a few changes as they draft. Others make changes constantly. Others leave all changes until the end of the first draft.

Here are a few ideas which many people find useful at the first draft stage.

Remember: Some of the exercises ask you to continue with writing you began in Unit 1, Preparing to write.

Ideas

USING THE WRITING SPACE

It is important at this stage to be able to see clearly what you have written and what changes you have made. So:
— Write on every second line. Make changes on the blank line above your writing.
— Write on every second page (if using an exercise book) or leave a wide margin (if writing on sheets of paper). Use this space for rough wording, comments, spelling attempts, and markings (arrows, etc.).
— Cross out rather than use typing fluid or a rubber. Then you can see your original wording or spelling. You may need these if you change your mind again.

e.g. Using the writing space in drafting a letter of protest:

> The principal has asked me ~~I would like~~ to write and
>
> protest about the proposed changes to [?]
>
> *I have lived in the area* traffic in Knox St. ✓As I understand it,
>
> *for 5 years* the street is to become two-way
>
> *and so I feel I know.* again. This is a ___? ___ step for ~~backward/regrettable~~
>
> *something about its* ~~traffic problems·~~ three reasons:

Exercise 1

Read the notes you made for exercise 1, Unit 1, *Preparing to write*. Use those ideas now to write a draft.
— Follow the advice about using space.
— Write as much as you like.
— Don't worry too much about correctness, but make any changes you want to.

GETTING STARTED

Getting started can be difficult even when you have prepared for writing. These ideas might help you.
— Don't worry too much about the beginning. You will often want to change it anyway. Try to get past it and keep going.
— Write a few different beginning sentences. Choose one and then continue writing. Even if you change your mind later, you will be on the way.
e.g. Getting started on the draft of a story:

That first day in Australia was the worst in my life.

I remember that day clearly – it was the worst in my life.

Of all days in my life, that first day was the worst.

— Don't begin at the beginning at all. Start anywhere. Come back later and write the beginning sentences.
e.g. Getting started on the draft of a letter of opinion for a class magazine:

I find it horrifying to see children travelling without seat belts — sometimes I even see them standing up or leaning out a window _ _ _ _ _ _ _ _ .

How careless and selfish some parents are!

Exercise 2

Look at this headline and picture. You are going to write something about it for a class magazine.

Christmas 100 years from now

HOW will our great-grandchildren celebrate Christmas? Scientists have been making a few educated predictions about the sort of festivities that will be enjoyed 100 years from now and if they're correct, there will certainly be some changes.

– Begin by brainstorming or by talking about it with other students.
– Start writing your draft. Keep in mind the points above.

KEEPING GOING

It is a good idea to push yourself to the end of a first draft. The important thing at this stage is to get your ideas on paper. If you stop to correct yourself too much, you may interrupt the flow of ideas.
— If unsure of the spelling of a word:
  ○ make an attempt and keep going
  ○ leave a space and keep going.
— If unsure of punctuation:
  ○ make an attempt and keep going
  ○ put a dash (—) in the trouble spot and keep going.
— If unsure about the words to use:
  ○ write two or three alternatives and keep going
  ○ leave a space and keep going
  ○ write it in your first language and keep going.
— Clearly mark any problem area for attention when you revise (see next unit).
e.g. Drafting a letter to the editor of a class magazine:

> I am disgusted (stunned) (?) to hear the
> news about recent class(es) cuts in
> this school. I cannot bel—ve (do not)
> that the government (government) could be so
> —?—. Education for all of us (everyone)
> is obv—sly (clearly) the most important
> expendit— (?) the government has
> — without education we are lost.
> Surely we can do something (take action).

— If you run out of ideas:
  ○ Look back to your preparation notes.
  ○ Read out loud what you have written so far or ask someone else to do this while you listen.
  ○ Begin to rewrite or type up what you have written.
  ○ Put your writing away for a time (an hour, a day, a few days). Return to it with a fresh and clear mind.

Exercise 3

Read the speed writing you did in exercise 2, Unit 1, *Preparing to write*. Write a first draft based on your speed writing. Try to keep going until the end of the draft.

Exercise 4

Use your notes for 'wh' questions from exercise 3, Unit 1, *Preparing to write*. Write a draft, keeping in mind the points above.

Additional exercises

Exercise 5

In exercise 9, Unit 1, *Preparing to write*, you made notes for a letter to a friend. Write a draft of that letter now, using your notes. Keep in mind all the points made in this unit.

Exercise 6

In exercise 10, Unit 1, *Preparing to write*, you made notes for a piece of writing. Use those notes now to write a first draft.

Exercise 7

In exercise 11, Unit 1, *Preparing to write*, you prepared for something you personally needed to write. Make a draft now.

3 *Revising*

Introduction

The revising stage is where you check that:
- you have said what you wanted to say
- you have said it in a clear and appropriate way.

Revising might take place while you are drafting or after you have finished a draft (your first, second or twentieth draft!).

This unit looks at some of the changes you might make and suggests ways to make your revising more effective.

Before you begin, think about these points:
○ Revising is the most important stage in the writing process.
○ It involves checking that your *content* and *purpose* are clear and appropriate for your *reader*, in the particular writing *situation*.
○ It is not just a matter of checking spelling, punctuation and grammar. It involves arranging, changing, adding, leaving out words, and so on.
○ It is a constructive part of the writing process and it is important that you see it in this way. You should give it some time and attention in *all* your writing. In a quick note to a friend you may not worry too much about punctuation, but you do want to make sure your message is clear.

Note: Exercise 2 asks you to continue with writing you have been working on in Units 1 and 2.

Ideas

SOME CHANGES YOU MIGHT MAKE WHEN REVISING

Look at the changes this writer made when revising a letter of complaint. They will help you when revising your own writing. She:
1. changed the order of parts to make the content or purpose clearer
2. added parts (especially to link ideas)
3. took out parts which were unnecessary
4. said the same thing in a different way
5. substituted one word for another
6. combined two or three sentences into one, by taking out unnecessary words or phrases
7. made very long sentences into two or three shorter ones

8. changed parts which were inappropriate for the situation, the purpose or the audience (too friendly and informal, too formal, etc.)
9. corrected grammar
10. changed the punctuation
11. corrected spelling.

---

6 Talbot St,
Coolgardie
17/10/88

Quick-Order Pty Ltd,
12 Stanley St,
Perth

① *On July 17th I ordered 3 books from your July catalogue. It is now October 17th, and they have not arrived.*

Dear Sir/Madam,

② *The books were "A Town like Alice" "Eureka" and "The Outback".*

It is now October 17th and I have been waiting for 3 books to arrive which I ordered from the July catalogue on July 17th. ~~to arrive.~~

Enclosed with that order was a cheque for $30 dollars to cover the cost of goods ③ ~~packaging~~ ⑩ and postage.

④ *The advertisement said* ~~You said in the advertisement~~ that I ~~can~~ *could* ⑨ expect to wait 6 weeks for delivery. I *have now* ⑨ waited twice that long *so* ② ⑩ I believe you owe me an apology and an explanation.

I had been looking for these particular books for months as a birthday present for a friend, and so I was extremely disappointed when they did not arrive in time. ⑧

The books were for my boyfriend's birthday. They had been difficult to find and exactly what he wanted. Unfortunately I told him about them and so he was very disappointed when they did not arrive in time. So was I. *by your unbusinesslike behaviour* ④

I am very surprised ~~about all this~~ as I ⑨ *have* ordered things many times ⑩ from your company over the years, and generally the service has ⑦ been prompt and ~~polite~~ *courteous* ⑤ ~~and as~~ *As* I live in the country I rely *greatly* on your mail order firm ⑩ *and* so I would like very much to continue my dealings with you.

⑥ Please notify me ~~imediately~~ *immediately* ⑪ of the expected date of delivery/ ~~I would also like an explanation~~ *and the reason* for the delay up to this point.

If I do not hear from you within 14 days, I ⑪ will ~~cansel~~ *cancel* my order and seek legal ~~advise~~ *advice* to recover the money owed to me.

Yours sincerely,

Exercise 1

a) Below is a draft of a club notice. The writer has forgotten to include this important information:
   - The display will be held on Saturday, 28th November at 8p.m.
   - It will be at the north end of the oval.
   - Children are free.
   - Members can bring friends.

   – Decide which is the best place for the information to go.
   – Rewrite the notice, making any changes you think necessary (e.g. combine sentences, take out words).

> **NORTHERN SUBURBS SOCCER CLUB**
>
> **FIREWORKS DISPLAY**
>
> The Club will hold a fireworks display at the end of the month. It will celebrate our 10th anniversary! The display will be held at the O'Connell Oval.
>
> All members are welcome to attend. There will be a small charge of $2 per person to cover food and drink. If you are coming, please tell the Secretary by 20th November.

b) Read this sports report which was written for a class magazine. Improve it by adding the linking words below it. You may use each word more than once.

Last Monday the Socceroos played in Birmingham against Aston Villa. They played well. Luck was not on their side. They were defeated. That was their first defeat in this world tour. They must play five or six more games in the UK and Europe. They return home on September 19th. Their next match is against Manchester United. This is expected to be a close match. The Socceroos are tipped to win.

and   before   however   but   although

c) Revise this short letter by taking out some unnecessary words or phrases. Keep the content the same.

26 January

Dear Eddie,
Here in Perth where I am at the moment, it's sunny and warm. I arrived yesterday afternoon at 3pm and already have a suntan. It's a nice change from the cold grey days at home. The hotel I am staying in is very close to the beach. Fortunately, I was lucky enough to get a room with a view. I expect to be here till the end of the month. Then I'll get the train across to Sydney. See you then —
        Lee

d) Read this paragraph from a story. Replace the words underlined with other words which say the same thing. The first one has been done for you.

> Suddenly they heard the phone ringing (the phone rang). The mother ran to get it. The family waited without speaking. They could barely hear her when she finally spoke. 'Willy, it's for you.' He hesitated for a second and then roughly took the phone out of her hand. He listened for a long while. His face showed no emotion. At last he spoke, but they were unable to understand the words. Suddenly he slammed down the receiver, got his coat and departed without a word.

e) There is too much repetition in these extracts from personal letters. Replace some words and phrases with words from the list provided. You may not need to use them all, and you may want to use some of them more than once. (Keep in mind that we usually write the name of a person, place or thing the first time we mention them).

it	him	them	she
there	hers	we	they
he	here	ours	one

i)   *Has Jana rung you from Newcastle? I have a feeling Jana has not got your number so here is Jana's — 049 621 723. Jana and Simon will be in Melbourne on approximately 17th Dec. What a shame you're not in Melbourne too. Jana and Simon would love to see you, I know.*

ii) *I am checking my report now and think the report will be finished by Christmas. I can't quite believe I'll be finished!!*

iii) *Thanks for the video. We haven't actually got a video machine yet but perhaps we'll have to get a machine now.*

iv) *Perhaps we'll come for a holiday to Darwin sometime if you are still in Darwin.*

f) Rewrite each pair of sentences below as one sentence. There may be more than one way to do this.
   i) *Personal letter*
      I'm glad to hear that you are well. I'm glad everything is going well with the business.
   ii) *Job application*
      I have enjoyed working here for the past three years. Now I'm looking for a change from hotel work.
   iii) *Letter of protest*
      I was particularly upset. My young children were watching TV at the time.
   iv) *Personal letter*
      Like me, he is from the south. We have something in common.
   v) *Formal letter*
      Please find enclosed a cheque for $18. It is the deposit for the workshop on August 23rd.

g) These sentences are very long. Divide each into two or more sentences. (You may need to add, leave out or change some words.)
   i) *News report for a school magazine*
      A severe thunderstorm passed through Sydney around noon yesterday, flooding some city streets, disrupting traffic and causing widespread damage especially in the Hurstville area where many trees were uprooted, roofs blown off and power lines brought down.
   ii) *Letter of opinion*
      Given the extent of the shoplifting problem these days, I think it is quite reasonable for store management to carry out bag searching, but I do think it is essential that there are warning signs and that the searches are done in a polite way and if this is done, customers have no cause for complaint.

IDEAS FOR MORE EFFECTIVE REVISING

- Read your writing out loud to yourself or have someone else read it to you. Often it is easier to *hear* parts that need revision.
- Ask someone else to read through your writing and to discuss it with you. Ask him or her, for example:
  o Which parts are unclear? Why? How can they be made clearer?
  o Are any words used wrongly or inappropriately? What other words could be used?
  o Which parts are the most interesting? Why?
  o Is the order of ideas clear or confusing?
  o Are any parts unnecessary?
- If you are working alone, put yourself in the place of the reader and ask yourself the same sorts of questions.
- Divide up the revising task. Only look for one or two things at a time.
- Clearly mark all the parts that need revision as you read. You may not be

able to change everything immediately, so you need to know where to return to.

— Become more aware of your own particular problem areas. Be on the lookout for them when you revise.

Exercise 2

Choose two or more pieces of writing you did in Units 1 and 2 to take to final draft stage. Revise as necessary using the ideas in this unit. Rewrite the pieces neatly when you have finished.

WRITING SUB-SKILLS

4 *Spelling*

Do not attempt to work through this unit in one session. You may not need to do all the exercises. It depends on whether or not you have problems with spelling.

Introduction

This unit will help you to:
— identify spelling errors
— spell unfamiliar words
— remember spellings
— become more aware of spelling.

Here are a few points to think about before you begin.

○ Spelling is visual. We *see* if a spelling is right or wrong. We remember the way it *looks*. Therefore, strategies which reinforce the visual image will help you most.
○ There is no single magical spelling method. Most people use a variety of strategies.
○ You yourself must develop an awareness of whether your spellings are right or wrong. Don't always depend on a dictionary or another person.
○ Correct spelling is more important in some writing (e.g. a job application) than in others (e.g. a short note to a friend).
○ *Revising* is the right time to look closely at your spelling. Don't worry about it too much while *drafting*. (See Units 2 and 3.)

Ideas

IDENTIFYING ERRORS

Being able to identify spelling errors is the first step to improving your spelling.
Whenever in doubt about a word:
— Ask yourself 'Does it look right?'
— Try to remember where you have seen it before and how it looked there.

- Look in other sections of your writing. You may have used it correctly already.
- When *drafting*, underline any words you suspect are wrong and keep going.
- When *revising*, do the same, but this time try to correct them.

Exercise 1

Give yourself about five minutes to write down any thoughts about the picture below. Make an attempt at spellings you aren't sure about and keep going.

(*Note*: We are only concerned here with identifying spelling errors, so don't worry too much about other things such as full sentences, punctuation, etc.)

Voices raised in anger

When you finish, look through your writing, and underline any spellings you think may be wrong.

Keep your writing for exercise 2.

SPELLING UNFAMILIAR WORDS AND CORRECTING ERRORS

When you are trying to write a word you are not sure of, or when you are trying
to correct a word you have identified as wrong, these strategies are useful:
— Make yourself write the word quickly. The correct spelling may come to you
automatically.
— Write it a few different ways to see which one looks right.
e.g.

Tursday   definitly
Thusday   definetly
Thursday ✓   defineatly
Thirsday   definitely ✓

— Write the part you are sure of and leave a blank for the difficult part. Try
different ways to fill in the blank.
e.g.

exp ____ nce ?   experience ✓
                           expereance
                           expiriance
                           experiance

— Think of other words that might have the same spelling pattern.
e.g.

slight   ?   right
                  might
                  fright .

— Use parts of other words you know.
e.g.

inflation ?   station
                  nation .

– Think of other words connected in meaning.
  e.g.

medi _ne ?   medi**c**al
                          medi**c**are

si _n ?   si**gn**al
                          si**gn**ature

– Break the word into chunks.
  e.g.

yes/ter/day   str/eng/then
horr/if/y/ing   dis/gust/ing

– Don't rely on the sound of the word as a major or first strategy. However, *after you have tried the above strategies* you can ask yourself: 'Have I got one or more letters for every sound I can hear?' (This is especially useful with long words.)
  e.g.

~~frighted~~   ~~nationalty~~
frightened ✓   nationality ✓

~~cuture~~   ~~crowed~~
culture ✓   crowded ✓

– Generally speaking, use the dictionary *after* you have tried these strategies.
– If using the dictionary, write down what you do know of the word, or write down some likely spellings first. This will make your search easier and lead you more quickly to spelling independence.
  e.g.

ach __v_ ?   achieve

disision ?
dicision ?   decision
decision ?
desision ?

Exercise 2

This is a continuation of exercise 1.
– Use any of the strategies above to correct the errors you identified there.
– Use the dictionary to confirm whether your spellings are right or wrong.
– Keep your writing for exercise 4.
(It is not essential to keep working on this piece of writing, but you can if you wish.)

Exercise 3

a) Use the dictionary to find out what these words are. Before looking, write down a few possibilities.

h..ght	fl..n.y
pat..nt	p.rs..t
em..gen.y	d.sp.r.te
det..g..t	brea..e

b) Use the dictionary to find the silent letters in these words.

lis.en	forei.n
c.aos	ve.icle
ca.m	dou.t
w.ether	recei.t

c) Some dictionaries help you with adding endings to base words. See if your dictionary can help you with adding -ed or -ing to these words.

apply	budget	change
occur	pay	tie
shop	believe	dance

REMEMBERING SPELLINGS

The strategies here will help you use your memory in the most effective way.
– Aim to remember the way a word *looks*. Put it into your memory as a visual unit.
– Don't just copy a word a number of times in order to remember it. This is passive and ineffective.
– Instead, memorize actively. Use a system like this:

Step 1 Study the word. Look at it as a whole, not as individual letters. Then look at the difficult part.

Step 2 Close your eyes or look away from the word and imagine it written. Imagine it in big letters, or in colour. It may help to see it big and then see it small. Focus on the difficult part.

Step 3 When you are ready, cover the word and write it. Decide if it looks right or wrong.

Step 4 Check it.

Step 5 If it is right, write the word again to be sure. If wrong, begin again. Do this as often as you need to.

Step 6 Write the word again – an hour later, a few hours later, a day later, a week later. Use it as often as you can.

- Keep a personal dictionary of the words you have spelt wrongly and of words you want to remember. When you need one of these words, attempt it from memory first, then check with this dictionary.
- Lessen the load on your memory by grouping words in your mind.
  e.g.

antique   could   weight   two
unique   would   height   twelve
    should   twenty

worry   employed   strain
sorry   enjoyed   sprain

- Make up personal memory tricks.
  e.g. You may remember the 'u' in 'Thursday' because your uncle rings you every Thursday.
  You may remember that 'e' comes before 'i' in neighbour because 'next' begins with 'ne' ('next door neighbour').
- Don't focus on individual letters when memorizing. Look at clusters of letters. This will build up your knowledge of likely English letter sequences.
  e.g.

fre-qu-ent   str-e-tch   t-aught

thr-ough   pro-test   Kn-ow-l-edge

- When you are copying a word (e.g. from a dictionary or a blackboard) do not copy one or two letters at a time. Look at the whole word and then try to write it without looking again.

Exercise 4

Use the six-step system to learn the words you spelt wrongly in exercise 1. Start a personal dictionary with those words.

Exercise 5

Try out the six-step system on these tricky words:

comfortable	breakfast
business	believe
necessary	neighbour
knowledge	because
guess	tomorrow
especially	separate

BECOMING MORE AWARE OF SPELLING

An important part of improving spelling is becoming more aware of the way words are spelt.
— Read as much as possible.
— Take notice of spellings.
   e.g. ○ Set aside a few minutes after you read a newspaper article to look closely at words that interest you.
       ○ Pay attention to words continually flashed at you on the TV screen.
       ○ Look at the words on signs around you when riding on public transport, or waiting in your car for the traffic lights to change.
— Play word games.You see them often in newspapers and magazines.
— Become more aware of your own spelling weaknesses. Check these whenever revising.

Exercise 6

a) Read this short article. When you have finished, go through it again and write down any words which interest you (e.g. those you know you can't spell, those you have never seen before, those that remind you of other words).

Sun is an enemy

Australia has one of the highest incidences of skin cancer in the world and even olive skinned people can die from skin cancer. In fact I've known of two beach inspectors in Manly-Warringah who have died as a direct result of skin cancer or melanoma in the past five years.

Don't get me wrong. A suntan is fine, but don't over-do it. Take your time, apply a good sunscreen and, if you have to be out in the sun for long periods over the hottest part of the day (generally between 11am and 3pm), take a hat and a shirt with you. It's important to have a break from the sun's harsh rays.

If you get painfully sunburned, apply a cool moist compress to the area, rest in a cool place and drink plenty of fluids — you may be dehydrated.

Do not break blisters. This could lead to infection. In serious cases seek medical attention.

Learn them using the ideas in this unit and then try to use them in some writing you are doing.

b) These words are from the article. Rewrite them, putting in the missing letters. (Try to do this first without looking back.)

in.iden...   p..nf...y
hi..est   sunb..ned
ski...d   inf...ion
pe.i.ds   s.ri..s
gen....ly   a..ent..n

5 Punctuation

Do not attempt to work through this unit in one session. You may not need to do all the exercises. It depends on whether or not you have problems with punctuation.

Introduction

In this unit, you will get *general* guidance only in the use of the most common features of punctuation. In Units 6–16, there are exercises to help you with punctuation in specific writing contexts.

Here are a few points to think about before you begin the exercises.

○ Punctuation helps your reader understand what you mean.
○ Punctuation helps you keep track of what you've written and of what you are going to write.
○ Some punctuation is simply convention. We do it now because it has always been done that way (e.g. capital letters, apostrophes).
○ *Revising* is the right time to look closely at your punctuation. Don't worry about it too much while *drafting*. (See Units 2 and 3.)
○ Looking at the punctuation used by other writers will help you more than learning rules.
○ Like everything else in writing, punctuation depends on your reader, purpose, content and situation.

In some kinds of writing you have more freedom than in others. Look at these two pieces of writing for example.

– Discuss the differences between the two pieces (in reader, purpose, content and situation).
– Discuss the differences in the type of punctuation used.

Dear Anna,
    See what you missed! Not quite as much snow as this however. Just went up the mountain — too cold for me and impossible to ski — blizzard conditions — exciting!
    Accommodation + food are fantastic. Sun's always out in the village (while the blizzard continues up above!)
    See you soon.
    Love Tania x

Miss Anna Barnado,
16/12 Slade St,
Annandale. 2038
N.S.W.

Reunion Dinner & Bush Dance:

Tickets available from the school, phone 416050 to book. Numbers are limited so please book early.

Cost: $21 per head.

Time: 7.00 for 7.30 start.

Table bookings optional.

Dress casual. Refreshments available.

DINE to a musical background
DANCE to RANG TANG BLOCK BAND

This is a once in 21 years celebration. Anyone associated with the school over the past 21 years is most welcome.

Book now. Phone 416050

Common features of punctuation

CAPITAL LETTERS

Use capital letters:
– to begin sentences
   e.g. We are happy to inform you that your application has been successful. Please contact us immediately about a suitable starting date.

– to begin proper names of people, places and things such as companies, government bodies, titles of books or films and important periods in history
   e.g. Mr Jackson
   Prime Minister
   River Nile
   Globe Insurance Company
   Department of Social Security
   'The Day of the Jackal' (capitals for important words only)
   World War II

– to begin days of the week and months of the year
   e.g. Friday, March

– to abbreviate groups of words which would have capitals if written out fully
   e.g. USA – United States of America
   ANU – Australian National University
   FCA – Finance Corporation of Australia

– *I* by itself or in a contracted form – *I'm, I've, I'd, I'll* – is always written as a capital.

Exercise 1

In this extract from a job application letter, the capital letters are left out. Insert them where necessary.

```
i wish to apply for the clerical position
advertised in the canberra times, saturday,
31st january. at present i am working for
the department of finance. although i have
only been there since november, i have
gained a wide variety of experience in
clerical duties. in addition, i worked for
the abc for one year as a pay clerk in
1984.
```

FULL STOPS

Use a full stop:
— at the end of a sentence
   e.g. Thank you for your letter dated 12/6/87. I am sorry that I have not
        responded before this.

— after an abbreviation (short form) *which does not end* with the last letter of
   the full form of the word
   e.g. Nov. 1986
        Prof. Jones
        $10 encl. (enclosed)

It's *not* necessary to use full stops in abbreviations like:
Dr (Doctor)
Mr (Mister)
St (Street)

Exercise 2

Put full stops and capital letters where needed into this short extract from a
brochure on 'Summer Safety'.

**What would you do if you
saw a snake?**

the safest thing to do is avoid it
snakes are naturally shy of humans
who are a threat to them their first
form of defence is to move away
from danger they will not
deliberately chase humans but if
provoked or cornered they may
attempt to bite snakes are
protected in all states and
territories of australia and may not
be killed unless they threaten life.

QUESTION MARKS

Use a question mark at the end of a sentence which is a question.
e.g.

Aping the young

Q: Why do older people like my brother, 56, try to ape young people in things like clothes, hair styles, music and speech?

I know that he isn't Robinson Crusoe by any means. But what is the reason for this sort of behaviour?

– Younger Sister (only 54)

Exercise 3

Put question marks where needed into this advertisement from a student news-paper.

W.I.R.E.

What is W.I.R.E.

It's a service by women for women. It's funded (given money) by the State Government.

Who needs W.I.R.E.

Any woman living in Victoria who needs help and advice.

For Example:

How can I stop my boss from annoying me.
Why am I finding it hard to get social security.
Where do I go for legal help.
What do I do if my ex-husband won't leave me alone.
Who can help me if my landlord threatens to evict me and my children.

Do I have to speak English to be understood on the telephone.

NO ! W.I.R.E has interpreters in your language.

In Melbourne
Ring 63 6841

In the Country
Ring (03) 637 838

Address
3rd Floor
238 Flinders Lane
Melbourne   3000

EXCLAMATION MARKS

Use an exclamation mark instead of a full stop:
— to emphasize your thoughts
— to express strong feelings (surprise, excitement, amusement, etc.).
You will use them most often in informal writing (letters to friends, postcards, notes, etc.).
e.g.

Right now I'm working at the Metropolitan
Museum of Art as a curator's assistant.
I'm loving it!

I got your note. I am very upset!!

I hear that you just had your
40th (!!!) birthday.

Exercise 4

Rewrite this message from a greeting card, replacing some full stops with exclamation marks.

Get well soon

Lex
    So sorry I haven't written sooner.
I heard about your accident from Ben.
What an amazing injury. Hope you are
following doctor's orders and staying in
bed. I won't be able to visit you for a
while. Business is booming. Thank
goodness. We've had so many bills to
pay. Hope the book cheers you up. I
absolutely loved it.
                            Love Julia

COMMAS

The comma has many uses. These examples will help you understand how to use it.

Barbara, please come back!

Other sources of Vitamin C are berry fruits, green vegetables, mangos, pawpaws, red and green peppers, parsley, oranges, lemons and grapefruit.

Jack, the fellow I told you about, has finally moved out.

A fourth concert, on February 2, has been added to those on January 28, 29 and 30.

In the end she told him off, and we all felt a lot better instantly.

For information about the programme, please phone 621035.

Exercise 5

Put commas where needed into this letter from the editor of a residents' newspaper.

Message from the Editor

This is the last issue of the Post before Christmas so I would like to take the opportunity of wishing readers a happy Christmas.

I would also like to take the opportunity to thank all those people who have helped the Post this year. These people give their time voluntarily to organise distribution letterbox write articles chase up information and advertisements take photographs and prepare the paper for the printer. I think you will agree they do a great job.

That's all for this year. See you in 1989.

The Editor

APOSTROPHE OF POSSESSION

The apostrophe of possession (') tells us that somebody or something 'owns' or 'possesses' something or somebody.

The underlined parts in the examples below are the 'owners'. Studying these examples will help you understand where to put the apostrophe.

Examples:

the flat of <u>John</u> – <u>John</u>'s flat
the boyfriend of my <u>sister</u> – my <u>sister</u>'s boyfriend
the car of my <u>boss</u> – my <u>boss</u>'s car
the friend of <u>Mr Jones</u> – <u>Mr Jones</u>'s friend
the school of my <u>nephews</u> – my <u>nephews</u>' school
the rights of the <u>workers</u> – the <u>workers</u>' rights
the centre of/for <u>the children</u> – <u>the children</u>'s centre
the liberation of <u>women</u> – <u>women</u>'s liberation

Can you see the rule?

The apostrophe (') comes immediately after the word that names the owner or owners (John, sister, boss, Mr Jones, nephews, workers, children, women). This is so for singular and plural nouns.

So:
– You add *'s* to singular nouns (John's, sister's, boss's, Mr Jones's).
– You add an *'* to regular plural nouns (nephews', workers').
– You add an *'s* to irregular plural nouns (children's, women's).

Note: Some singular nouns end in an 's' sound (boss, Mr Jones). It is usual to treat these as other singular nouns and add *'s*. Some writers, however, add an apostrophe *only* to some of these nouns, especially if the word will have too many 's' sounds (e.g. the car of Mr Janssens – Mr Janssens' car) and if it is a biblical or classical name (the journey of Moses – Moses' journey, the poems of Keats – Keats' poems).

Exercise 6

Change these examples so that you use the apostrophe of possession.

a) the father of my boyfriend
b) the brother of Peter
c) the house of my friends
d) the association of students
e) the office of the foreman
f) the changing room of the men
g) the office of Ross
h) the club of the sportswomen

APOSTROPHE OF OMISSION

The apostrophe of omission tells us that letters are missing. Look at the examples below.
The underlined letters can be replaced with an apostrophe. (What is unusual about the
last example?)
Examples:
what is — what's
let us — let's
are not — aren't
she is/she has — she's
I would/I had — I'd
cannot — can't
will not — won't
Most people use short forms, with the apostrophe, in informal writing (notes,
postcards, personal letters, etc.).

Exercise 7

Use short forms for all the underlined words in the note below.

> Hi,
>   Just writing to say I <u>might not</u> go to
> Geelong for the long weekend so maybe <u>I
> will</u> get to see you after all. <u>I have</u> tried
> to contact Jack about your staying there
> but he is never there If I <u>cannot</u> get him,
> <u>you will</u> have to spend money on a long
> distance phone call. (I know how <u>that</u>
> <u>will</u> hurt!)
>   Hope <u>all is</u> well with you.
>   Bye Lien

INVERTED COMMAS OR QUOTATION MARKS

Use double quotation marks (" "):
— When you write down the exact words someone says (direct speech).
   e.g.

I finally got the chance to say "Follow that cab!"
It was just like the movies!

– When you write the name of a book, a play, a film, etc.
    e.g.

John just loved "The History of Rock and Roll".
He sends his thanks.

Use single quotation marks (‘   ’) if you use titles or direct speech within direct speech.
    e.g.

His exact words were "I am going to write a book.
I'm calling it 'How to Manage your Parents'."

(You sometimes see the reverse situation, but in handwriting this still seems to be the rule.)

Exercise 8

Use quotation marks where needed in this draft of a story.

```
I couldn't let her go without a word. Will you return?
I asked. Never, was the short reply. She saw the
distress on my face. Look, she said, I don't mean to
hurt you. I just can't see any other way. It seems
hopeless. I knew she was right.
```

BRACKETS

Use brackets:

– *within a sentence* to separate a thought that is extra to the main idea of a sentence
– *within a longer piece of writing* to separate a sentence or sentences that are extra to the main idea.
    e.g.

I'm really interested in setting up a community craft shop (like the one we saw that weekend).

I went into hospital on Xmas Eve, had Meredith on Xmas morning, and was home on Boxing Day. (A three-day stay in hospital is considered a long time here.)

We have been asked (told) to do 3 nights a week overtime!

⟫→

Jumble Sale

SATURDAY, 8th OCTOBER, 1988

9.00a.m. to 2.00p.m.

AT HENRY LAWSON HOUSE
(OLD REVESBY WORKERS' CLUB PREMISES)
BRETT STREET, REVESBY

Exercise 9

Use brackets where appropriate in the writing below.

TERESA

Boss wants to see you when you come in it sounds urgent.

Ingrid

Dear Jan,

We've been in Canberra now for 3 months. It is freezing at the moment —6° this morning but we like it a lot.

DASHES

Use dashes:
- in informal writing instead of full stops, commas, brackets
  e.g.

Fran
This is THE place for a holiday — sun, surf, good food, etc etc. I'm not really sure when I'll be back — maybe never — do you want to join me? Write c/- Poste Restante — same as before — oh well — back to the beach (yawn!)
Phil x

F. Marco
6 Reid Place
Braddon A.C.T.
AUSTRALIA

– in formal writing, to separate items listed.
   e.g.

> Things you can do to lose fat:
> – increase level of exercise
> – decrease calorie intake, but avoid crash diets
> – eat larger meals at the start of the day, smaller meals at the
>   end
> – record your eating habits.

Exercise 10

Rewrite this extract from a brochure on 'Summer Safety'. Use dashes and other punctuation to make it clearer.

> Are you planning to go into the bush this summer remember to take a safety kit which contains a map and compass waterproof matches in a waterproof container solid fuel firelighter or candle a whistle a mirror for emergency signalling a small notebook and pencil a knife or other sharp instrument a cup or container water sterilization tablets a first aid kit a torch

COLONS(:) AND SEMI-COLONS (;)

These features of punctuation are often used incorrectly. It is probably best to avoid them. Here are examples of their correct usage.

> ### Better Photography
>
> Here are some important points to remember when taking a photo:
> avoid having your subjects look at the camera
> avoid group photos where everyone has the same smile
> learn to take photos without being seen.
>
> Going on holidays? Before you set off, check your camera carefully. Make certain everything is in good working order; shoot a trial film to be sure. Estimate how many films you will need; nothing is more irritating than being out of film in the midst of perfect scenery. Also, don't forget your lens cap; you'll need it to keep unwanted light out of your camera.

Exercise 11

Imagine you are on the editorial committee of a student magazine. Your job is to edit the front page below for punctuation.

The Times

OCTOBER/NOVEMBER

Editorial

On the last sunday of october the clocks are changed in most of australia.

In all states except for queensland and western australia clocks and watches are put forward by one hour. For example 9 in the morning becomes 10. we call this daylight saving because we make better use of the increased daylight hours in the longer summer days People can enjoy sporting and outdoor activities until quite late each evening.

Enjoy the extra daylight while it lasts because on the first sunday of march, everyone will have to put the hands of their watches and clocks back again, and get up in the dark

See you next edition

Lygon Street Festa

The lygon street festa takes place on Saturday the 11th and Sunday the 12th of November in Carlton. There are many Italian shops and cafes in lygon street so the festa has an Italian flavour.

However many other ethnic groups take part in the two days of celebrations There is music dancing and all kinds of food as well as fun and games for the kids. You can get free programs on the day.

But one warning. If you want a quiet weekend then stay at home! You'll find almost as many people in this one street as at the Melbourne Cup

Melbourne Cup

Australias greatest horse racing event is held on the first Tuesday in november at flemington race course and the distance is 3200m 2 miles Melbourne is the only place in the world that has a public holiday for a horse race.

The first Cup was run in 1861. That year there were 17 horses in the race and 4,000 people attended. These days there are about 25 horses running and often more than 100,000 people at the Melbourne Cup many more thousands of people stay home and watch it on television or listen to it on the radio.

Working in pairs where possible, correct the punctuation where you think necessary. (You may need to add punctuation, omit it or change it from one form to another.)

Compare your results with those of other students.

Part 2: Context units

FUNCTIONAL WRITING CONTEXTS

6 Postcards

Introduction

You may write postcards for many different purposes, for example:
– to tell someone about your holiday or trip.
– to let someone know travel details.
– to tell someone your new address or telephone number.
– to send news about friends or family.
– to ask for news of friends or family.
– to send a greeting (e.g. for a birthday or New Year).
– to remind someone to write to you.
– to let someone know you are thinking of them.

Collect some examples of postcards amongst the students in your class. They will be useful in many of the exercises in this unit.

Read the two postcards below. Discuss each writer's purpose (or purposes) for sending the card. Choose from the list above or add others.

Dear Marcia,
   This is mainly to give you my new London address.
   19 Burma Rd.
   London N 16
   U.K.
Haven't heard from you in quite a while – your turn you know. Better still – when are your holidays? Visit me!!
      Love Amanda
            xxx

Marcia Molehaven

2/119 Stamford St.

Parkside

S.A. 5063

AUSTRALIA

⟫→

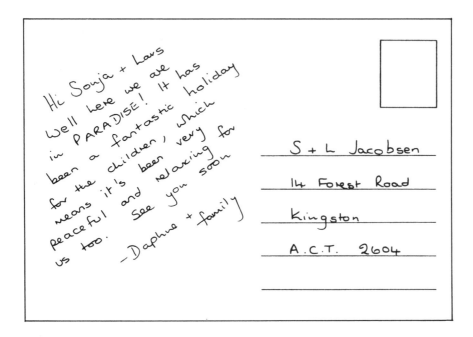

The postcard message reads:

Hi Sonja + Lars

Well here we are. It has been a fantastic holiday in PARADISE! for the children, which means it's been very relaxing and peaceful for us too. See you soon

— Daphne + family

S + L Jacobsen
14 Forest Road
Kingston
A.C.T. 2604

Keep these points in mind when writing postcards.

i) Because postcards are informal and personal, you may begin and end in any way you like.

ii) Because there is not much space you usually:
   – mention just a few things
   – use shortened sentence forms.

iii) You do not have to follow strict rules of punctuation. For example, you may use dashes (–) instead of full stops or commas to separate ideas.

Exercise 1

a) The postcard messages below need some punctuation to make them clear. Copy out each one, adding dashes and full stops where it is necessary to divide ideas.

   i) Beautiful isn't it it really looks like the picture too green hills and blue sky as far as the eye can see we are staying in an old farmhouse which has been turned into a small hotel very comfortable I'm in no hurry to leave.

   ii) I hope you are still having a good time in Italy Angela gave me her sister's address to send to you she said to visit her when you are in Ancona it's 48 Via Fontana her name is Luisa Vincenza stay in touch.

b) It is important to address your postcard clearly and accurately, in spite of the story (top of page 49) that appeared in a local newspaper.
   Use the postcards in the Introduction as models to set out the following addresses. Add capital letters where necessary.

   i) 6/697 military road mosman NSW 2088 australia

   ii) 22 north street heidelburg victoria 3084

   iii) flat 5 17 mitchell road sandy bay tasmania 5007

   iv) 81 wesley drive titirangi new zealand

Postie beats a challenge

Peter Ashby, who lives at Unit 10, 228 Campbell Parade, Bondi Beach, would like to thank the Bondi Beach Post Office for the prompt delivery of his mail. This postcard from Germany arrived at his home address. It bore the following address: P. Asby, Sydney – NSW – BONDI BEACH. UNIT 5 OR 6. No – approx 28–36 – next to RSL Club – 11 Haus – before white sailing boot on 2 double garage doors. Australia. Postman – if you can't find it, deliver – please to Bondi Iceberg Club.

Exercise 2

To emphasize words or expressions in a postcard you can use:
– capital letters
– underlining
– exclamation marks.
a) Look at examples in the postcard below.
   Find other examples in the postcards in the Introduction.

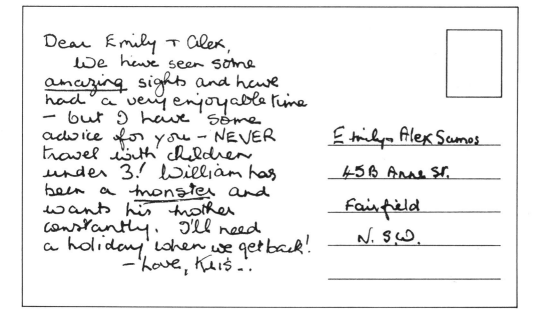

⋙→

b) Rewrite the postcards below, emphasizing some words or expressions.
   Compare your ideas with those of other students.

i)

Dear Hugh
        Just a short note
to say - happy birthday.
I hope you have a wonderful
day and I'm sorry I won't be
there to help you celebrate -
maybe next year - who knows?
All the best
              Bonnie

ii)

Dear Lon

Here I am in
New York. It's wild
and crowded and
crazy but I love
it.
        See you soon
           X David

Exercise 3

a) Take note of the words left out in the examples below.

We arrived here on June 2nd.	→	Arrived here June 2nd.
I went for a 20km walk today so I am exhausted now.	→	Went for 20km walk today so am exhausted now.
We are leaving on the late train tomorrow.	→	Leaving late train tomorrow.
It has been fantastic for the children.	→	Has been fantastic for the children.

b) Rewrite the postcard below using shortened sentences.
   Compare your shortened sentences with those of other students.

I'm having a great time. I wish you could be
here. I'm staying in a small boarding house
near the lake. It's a very friendly place. I
plan to stay here till early in August and then
I'll fly to Adelaide. Are you still able to put
me up for a while? I hope so. I'll contact you
again before I leave.

Exercise 4

Imagine you are away on a holiday. You have written this short personal letter to a friend. You now decide to send a postcard containing similar news to another friend.

Change the letter to fit onto a postcard. Mention all the main topics but shorten some sentences and leave out some information.

Dear Carla,

Unfortunately our holiday is almost over. We've had the most wonderful 3 weeks. The weather has been just great. I think it has only rained once — and the rest of the time we've had bright sunshine.

We've spent all day, every day, outside — either at the beach or bush-walking or going for drives into the hills. One day we walked about 10km along the coast. It's wonderful scenery, with rocky cliffs and little sandy beaches. Jan has taken lots of photos so we can show you when we get back.

The sunsets are magnificent too. Every evening we sit on the beach and admire the wonderful colours in the sky — and then when it gets dark, there are so many stars in the sky. You never see that in the city!

But as I said, unfortunately it's nearly over. We'll be leaving on Saturday. I'll give you a ring when we get back — lots of love,

Miriam

Exercise 5

In this exercise you are asked to make two lists of useful words. Follow these steps:
— Write as many words as you can.
— Don't worry about careful spelling as you write.
— When you finish, underline any spellings you are not sure of.
— Try to correct them using the ideas in Unit 4, *Spelling*.
— Finally, check them in your dictionary.

a) In postcards you often use descriptive words to show you like something or someone (e.g. wonderful, great, fabulous). Make a list starting with the words you find in previous exercises.
b) Sometimes you have a holiday where nothing goes right. Make a list of words you could use to describe such a holiday. Think about the weather (e.g. miserable), the people (e.g. unfriendly), the accommodation (e.g. crowded).

Exercise 6

Complete the postcards below. Begin by discussing your ideas with other students.

i) *Hi everyone,*

    We've had a great 2 weeks holiday

    here. ....

    ....

    ....

    We'll be sorry to leave.
    See you soon.

                      Love Jill.

ii) .... ,

....

....

I've been so busy since I arrived,
finding a job and somewhere to live.
Now I'm beginning to feel settled.
Before I forget, here is my new address
— 2/12 Burton St, Hove, 5048.

....

....

Exercise 7

Think about a holiday that you enjoyed. Imagine that you are on that holiday now and are writing a postcard to someone you know. Follow these steps:
— Brainstorm for ideas (see Unit 1, *Preparing to write*) under some of these headings: place, weather, accommodation, things to do, people.
— Decide what you are going to mention. (There is probably not enough space to mention everything.)
— Write your message, keeping in mind all the features of postcard writing you have practised in this unit.

Exercise 8

Choose one or more of the following situations and write the postcard. Write more than one draft if you want to.
a) The holiday of your dreams has not turned out well. Everything has gone wrong. You write home to your family or class friends about it.
b) You are on holiday in a foreign country. In a postcard to a friend you mention one or two aspects of life that are interesting or unusual, and remind them to write to you.
c) Your holiday is coming to an end. A friend has promised to meet you at the station/airport when you arrive. You write and tell him or her the necessary information.
d) You have recently moved to another part of the country. You send a postcard explaining to some old friends how it is different, and telling them your new address.

Exercise 9

Buy a postcard of the city or town in which you live. Think of a friend overseas or interstate who would like to hear from you. Write the postcard and *send it*!

7 Notes and messages

Introduction

Discuss with other students the occasions when you have written notes to, or received notes from, any of the following people:
- friends
- family
- tradespeople
- people who work with you
- people who share your house
- teachers
- landlords or rental agents
- the public
- others.

Work in groups of two or three. Read the letter and the note below and discuss:
- What is the main purpose of each?
- How is the note different from the letter? (Think about the layout, content, the words and expressions used, the punctuation, etc.)
- Why are they different?

Compare your findings with those of other groups.

1/6/88.

Dear Gabrielle,

How are you? I hope you're not planning a holiday, because we're driving down for the long weekend and are hoping to see you.

We'll arrive on Thursday morning about 10.30 – will be staying at Dad's, but we'll call in to see you first. (Can't remember if you work Thursdays or not). If we don't catch you then, can you ring me at Dad's later. His number is 263907. We've got some things to do in the afternoon but should be back by 5.

Some old friends from Adelaide are coming to dinner on Saturday night and we'd love you to come too. Any chance? Sorry it's such late notice.

That's it then – leave all the news till the weekend.

Love
Kerry.

> GABRIELLE. Thurs. 11 am
>
> Guess who's in town? Staying at Dad's — ring me after 5 if *you* can (263907) Come to dinner Sat night ??
>
> Love
> Kerry.

When writing notes or messages:
i)   Write time and day/date if it is important.
ii) Emphasize the important words by using:
     – capital letters
     – underlining or other marking
     – punctuation.
iii) Leave out unnecessary words if you wish. Full sentences are not necessary especially in notes to friends and family members.
iv) Use dashes (–) instead of full stops, commas and even question marks if you wish. However, question marks are sometimes necessary to make your meaning clear.
v)   End in any way you like. Formal endings are not necessary. Usually your name is enough.

_____

Exercise 1

Look at the notes below. For each one discuss these questions:

a) When was it written? Is the time of writing important?
b) Where might you find it? Why do you think that?
c) What is its main purpose? How did the writer help to make this clear?
d) What is the relationship between the writer and the reader? How do you know?

> Sue,
>
> Going out to dinner tonight (again). May be "home" about 5pm to change.
>
> Jill (Thursday)

> Wed 11·30 am
> Luke Johnston
> Mark called. Ring him *tonight* between 9 and 10 — IMPORTANT
> Ian

SAT. AFTERNOON

MARIA & JO
        WHERE WERE YOU ??
YOU MISSED THE OPPORTUNITY OF THE YEAR —
TO ENTERTAIN YOUR MELBOURNE COUSINS.
        VERY DISAPPOINTING — RING YOU
SOMETIME SOON.
                BRANKO .

PLEASE wash your own cups .
We DON'T HAVE A DISHWASHER !

MESSAGE PAD			SUBJECT OR MESSAGE:
NAME: Kim F.	DATE: 20/2		Needs more information
	TIME: 11-45		about next week's
CALLER: Helena Peters			meeting.
OF:			What do you know?
TELEPHONE NO:	EXT:		
PLEASE PHONE		✓	
WILL PHONE AGAIN			Dorothy .
WILL RETURN			
PLEASE VISIT			
URGENT			
PAPERS ATTACHED			

Exercise 2

Make the notes below clearer and more interesting by using:
– capital letters
– extra marking (underlining, circling, heavy printing)
– punctuation (exclamation marks, question marks).
(Don't change any words.)
e.g.

DANGER
PLEASE DO NOT USE ⟶
TILL FURTHER NOTICE

＊ **DANGER!!** ＊

PLEASE DO NOT USE
TILL FURTHER
NOTICE.

＊   ＊

i)

> Attention. Parents who
> have not paid fees,
> please pay promptly.
> We're in the red
> again.

iii)

> Important – Ring your
> mother – Sounds upset
> – She rang 3 times
> before 7am.

ii)

> Please don't park
> here again as it is
> impossible for me
> to get out of my
> driveway. Thank you.

iv)

> How about a movie
> Friday night? Just the
> two of us. Please
> don't tell Rick.

Exercise 3

In the note below, there is no punctuation.
– Read it through first for understanding.
– Then write it out and add dashes (–) in pencil wherever you think they are
  needed.
– Go through it again and change some dashes into full stops, commas, question
  marks or exclamation marks. (Don't change any words.)

Wed 10 am

alan

patricia rang to ask me to leave you this note she tried to call you but there was no answer she said to tell you that her plane wont get in till 10 pm not 9 pm as she thought she still wants you to meet her if you cant can you leave a message at the airport

josie

Exercise 4

In the note below, the writer leaves out many unnecessary words.
– Find examples of this and discuss what the full sentence is in each case.
– Discuss the sorts of words left out.

27/12

Ali & Iona,

① Welcome!

② Clean sheets on beds. Towels in cupboard under stairs.

③ We've taken best knives – hope others don't drive you mad.

④ All neighbours expecting you.

⑤ Back on 11th. See you then – please stay beyond then if necessary – plenty of room in attic!

⑥ Help yourselves to everything.

⑦ Have a good time and
Happy New Year!!

Liza.

P.S. Jane had a girl on 23rd. Yet un-named.

P.P.S. Corner store closes 7.30 p.m.

Find other examples in the notes in exercise 1.

Exercise 5

All the notes in this exercise are written to close friends or family members. Shorten them by leaving out all unnecessary words. (Change some words if you want to, and remember to use punctuation and other methods to make your notes clear.) Compare your notes with those of other students.

e.g. I've gone to the beach and won't be back until 5 o'clock.

> GONE TO BEACH – BACK AT <u>5</u>

a) Jenny rang at about 11 o'clock. She said to ring her before going to her place. She said it was urgent.

b) I have left the tools behind the garage door. Be careful of that very big spider in the left-hand corner – we think it might be dangerous. What do you think?

c) We've run out of everything. If you're hungry, there's some bread in the tin (it's a bit stale) and some Vegemite in the top cupboard. If you can't last till 10 o'clock get a take-away from the corner shop. I must fly now.

d) John called. There is a party tonight at 1/130 Blair St, Newtown. I'll be there at about 9 o'clock. It should be good. Can you bring some wine?

e) The camping trip is off. I'll call you later. It's too hard to explain now.

f) I'm sorry about this mess. I've been searching for 1½ hours for one pair of socks. I couldn't even find a dirty pair – what have you done with them all? I'll clean up the mess when I get back.

Exercise 6

a) Look at these two notes. The reason for writing is the same in both, but the wording is different.

> BILL
> <u>DON'T FORGET</u>
>
> Pick up dry cleaning
> – $3.50 to pay.
> Lina

> Chris
> Please pick up dry cleaning if possible. Could you pay the $3.50 owing? I'll pay you back tonight.
> Thanks Lina.

Discuss:
   i) the way they are different
   ii) what the relationships might be between the writer and the person written to
   iii) the connection between (i) and (ii).

b) Do the same for these two notes.

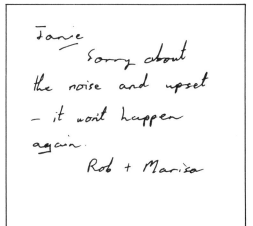

> Dear Liz,
>   Just a short
> note to apologize about
> the noise and upset.
>   I can assure you, it
> won't happen again. We're
> very sorry.
>   Rob + Marisa

> Jane
>   Sorry about
> the noise and upset
> — it won't happen
> again.
>   Rob + Marisa

c) Look at these two notes. In each case, the writer and the reader know each other very well.

i) Jack
    Don't go out till the
    plumber calls. Ring me
    with the bad news!!
        Paulo

ii) Angus,
    Remember, dinner at 8
    tonight. Don't be late!

        Geraldine

– Rewrite (i) for an older relative.
– Rewrite (ii) for a very new boyfriend.

Exercise 7

Telephone messages can be difficult because you have to change spoken language into written, and because you have to write quickly. Look at this conversation:

Caller:	It's Mary Simmons here. Is Susan there, please?
Receiver of call:	No, she's not, I'm sorry. She'll be here by 10 though. Can I take a message?
Caller:	Yes. I've been trying to call her for days now, but she never seems to be in. I really need to speak to her. Can you get her to ring me as soon as she comes in?
Receiver of call:	I'll be sure to give her the message.
Caller:	I was going to go out now but I'll wait for her call. Thank you very much.

Here are two ways to write the message:

Susan,
Mary Simmons rang. PLEASE RING HER NOW!!
Sounds very important. She's waiting for you to ring
before going out.
S.K. (9-30 Tues)

MESSAGE PAD			SUBJECT OR MESSAGE:
NAME: SUSAN	DATE: TUES		She's waiting for
	TIME: 9-30		you to call !!
CALLER: MARY SIMMONS			
OF:			
TELEPHONE NO:	EXT:		
PLEASE PHONE		✓	
WILL PHONE AGAIN			S.K.
WILL RETURN			
PLEASE VISIT			
URGENT VERY			
PAPERS ATTACHED			

Read the three telephone conversations below.
– Write a draft of the message you would write in each case.
– Revise the drafts as needed.
– Compare your messages with those of other students.

a) Caller: Is Mr Giorgi there?
   Receiver: No. It's his wife here. Can I help you?
   Caller: Yes. He rang about the electrical fittings, but I wasn't in. Can you tell him I'll bring them over tonight so he can choose the ones he wants.
   Receiver: I'll leave him a note 'cause I'm going out now. Thanks for calling. Bye.

b) Caller: It's Frank Woods here. Can you leave a note for Fred when he arrives? It's bad news, I'm afraid. Tell him that job is off. They gave it to some firm in Blackburn. I'll call back later with the details, or he can ring me before 2.30.
   Receiver: I'll give him the message, Mr Woods.

c) Caller: It's Hot Records here. I wanted to speak to Anna Demetrios.
   Receiver: I'm sorry, she won't be back till later this afternoon. Can I take a message?
   Caller: Yes, if you could tell her the order has arrived at last. It's my day off tomorrow but Lucy here knows all about it, so tell Anna to ask for her if she comes in then.
   Receiver: All right. I'll let her know. Bye.

Exercise 8

Make a list of any words that you had trouble spelling in the exercises in this unit. Use the techniques in Unit 4, *Spelling*, to learn them.

Exercise 9

Choose some of the situations below. Write the note or message required.

a) A friend is supposed to arrive at your house at 4.30 p.m. It is now 4.50 and you have to get to the post office before 5. You go out and leave a note on the door.
b) The washing machine has broken down. You have to go out but you leave a note for someone in the family to tell them not to use it.
c) You have a friend minding your house for a few days. You leave a note to tell her where some things are around the house and to remind her about feeding the cat and so on.
d) You visit some friends but find no-one home. You have some important news to tell them so you leave a note.
e) You are at work. A workmate's husband rings to say he'll meet his wife at 5.15 p.m. He doesn't say where, but he says to tell her not to be late. You leave a note for your workmate.
f) A handyman is coming to your house to do a number of small repairs. You leave a note about what needs to be done. (Think of what *really* needs to be done in *your* home.)
g) You are at work. There is a problem with some machinery. You leave a note about it for a co-worker.

Exercise 10

Think of some situations (at home, at work, at school) when you might need to write a note. Write those notes now. Prepare and draft as much as you need to.

8 Advertisements

Introduction

Have you ever needed to advertise in order to:
– buy something
– sell something
– hire someone
– find a job
– publicize a business
– publicize an event
– give information to the public
– ask for information from the public?

Look at the two advertisements below. Discuss:
– What is their common purpose?
– How are they different?
– Why are they different?

Office furniture, desk $100,
filing cabinet $95, swivel
chair $45, or $210 the lot.
As new cond. 45 1617.

<u>FOR SALE</u>
OFFICE FURNITURE
* Desk $100
* Filing cabinet (3 drawer) $95
* Swivel chair $45
<u>OR</u> $210 for the lot!!
All in as new condition.
Ring 45.1617 anytime

Keep these points in mind when writing advertisements:

i) Choose your first word carefully for a classified advertisement. The reader
    will use the first word to find what they want. It is usually the name of the
    item or service being advertised. (See the first advertisement above.)

ii) Keep classified advertisements short to reduce the cost. Shortened sentences and abbreviations can help.

iii) Make your advertisement for a window or notice-board stand out. (Use, for example, underlining or big print.)

iv) Draft and revise carefully, even if you send a classified advertisement by phone.

Exercise 1

a) Look at the two drafts of a classified advertisement below. In the second, the writer has shortened the advertisement to save cost. Take note of the sorts of words left out.

First draft: I do dressmaking and alterations for both
                 adults and children. I specialize in
                 making wedding gowns. My prices are very
                 reasonable. Please phone me on 349 1757.

Second draft: Dressmaking, alterations. Adults, children.
                 Specialize in wedding gowns. Reasonable
                 prices. 349 1757.

b) Rewrite the classified advertisements below to make them shorter. You may need to change some words and the order of some of the information.

i)   **LOST:** One pair of sunglasses, somewhere in the Westside shopping centre on Saturday morning. The glasses have a white frame and were in a green glasses case. There is a reward for anyone finding them. Please contact Sheri on 92 5487.

ii) I am a man in my early 50s. I am healthy, energetic and quite good-looking. I am very interested in travel. I would like to meet a sincere and kind woman, between 40 and 55 years old. If you would like to meet me, please write to Box B12, The Courier, 404 South Road.

iii) I am a young woman looking for share accommodation in the southern suburbs. I would prefer a house. I am friendly and a non-smoker. I have my own furniture. Please ring me after 6.00pm on 83 4549.

Exercise 2

Some newspapers ask you to send your advertisements by phone. Others provide forms to be filled in like the one below. Read it carefully to find out the conditions and costs involved. Work out the cost of your shortened advertisements from exercise 1 above.

Name ....

Address ....

.... P/Code ....

Phone No. (W) ....

(H) ....

PLEASE include point of contact such as address, phone number or P.O. Box number.

Classifieds

THE SURRY COSMOPOLITAN
P.O. BOX 627
DARLINGHURST NSW 2010
MINIMUM 10 words.
4 lines or 18 words $5.00 Additional words 25¢
INCLUDE YOUR CHEQUE OR POSTAL ORDER MADE PAYABLE TO THE SURRY COSMOPOLITAN

PRINT ONE WORD IN EACH SPACE

Exercise 3

Sometimes you may decide that it is better to pay more for a longer advertisement.

a) Compare the pairs of classified advertisements below. Discuss the advantages of the advertisements on the right.

CLEANING. Carpets, windows, Party clean-ups, etc. Ph. 445 8809.

CLEANING. We offer quality, comprehensive cleaning of homes, units and offices. We guarantee to beat the lowest reasonable quote you may have. Brighter Cleaning Service. Phone 555 2913. Let Brighter make it brighter!

Garage sale. 34 Wilson Ave, Penrith. Saturday. Household goods and furniture.

Garage sale. Bargains, bargains, bargains. You never know what treasures you may find. There are books, furniture, clothes, records, plants and more. We are moving and we must sell everything. Bring your money to 2 Chaplin Lane, Westmead. Sunday 8am.

b) Add more information to the classified advertisements below.

i) Mother of 2 will mind child. Ph. 333 8702.

ii) Odd jobs. Gardening, cleaning, rubbish removal. Ring Lee. 929 4761.

iii) Man wants to share flat/house. References available. Ring Andy 518745 or a.h. 287654.

Exercise 4

Abbreviations usually follow one of the patterns below:
- first letter of each syllable or part of a word
  e.g. s.c. — self-contained
- first letter of each word in an expression
  e.g. l.u.g. — lock up garage
- first few letters of a word (often the whole of the first syllable)
  e.g. mod. — modern
- first and last letters of a word
  e.g. rm — room
- letters from the beginning, middle and end of a word (usually consonants)
  e.g. cpts — carpets.

a) Below is an advertisement for a person to share a flat. Work out the meanings of the circled abbreviations.

PERSON to share 3 b.r house, Eastwood. Prefer professional female. Own furn. required, $65 p.w. bond plus expenses. Ph. 270 1810 wk/dys. 7.30–10 a.m. or aft. 9 p.m.; Sat. until 5 p.m.

b) Discuss ways to abbreviate the circled words in the advertisements below. Then check the list of common abbreviations at the end of this unit.

i)

● **Wanted To Rent**

House, 3 bedroom with garage. Close to transport and schools. References available. Phone after hours 72 3301.

ii)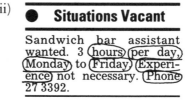

● **Situations Vacant**

Sandwich bar assistant wanted. 3 hours per day, Monday to Friday. Experience not necessary. Phone 27 3392.

Exercise 5

In the following FOR SALE advertisements the description of the item is missing. Think what a buyer would want to know and make up a brief description. Use some abbreviations if you like.

e.g. Bed queen-size, pine base and mattress, excellent condition.
....$200 o.n.o. Ph. 44 2266.

i) Child's bicycle ....
.... $40 a.h. 43 5678.

ii) Holden ....
.... $7,995. Any reasonable offer considered. 222 3722.

iii) Washing machine ....
.... Phone after 7pm 334 5545.

Exercise 6

a) Look at the changes this person made when writing a classified advertisement to find a childminder.

> WOMAN
> ~~PERSON~~ WANTED TO CARE FOR
> ~~SM~~ 10 MNTH OLD ~~IN MY~~ 2/3 HOURS
> ~~2 OR 3 TIMES A WEEK~~ TWICE WEEKLY
> IN MY HOME. WATSON. 415292

> KIND WOMAN WANTED TO CARE
> FOR 10 MONTH OLD BABY. APPROX
> 3 HOURS TWICE WEEKLY. PREFERABLY
> IN MY HOME. WATSON. 415292

b) Choose something from the following list that you personally would like help with.

gardening	bookkeeping	dressmaking
learning English	babysitting	catering
ironing	lawn mowing	typing
house cleaning	window cleaning	childminding

Follow these steps to write a Help Wanted advertisement:
– Write a draft.
– Revise your draft (adding extra information, crossing out unnecessary parts, abbreviating and punctuating as necessary).
– Write your advertisement out neatly.

Exercise 7

Imagine you have lost something valuable or very dear to you. You decide to put one advertisement in the Lost and Found classifieds and another in a shop window.

Use the examples below as a guide to write your advertisements.

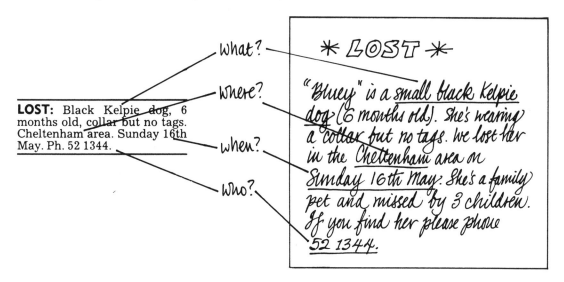

LOST: Black Kelpie dog, 6 months old, collar but no tags. Cheltenham area. Sunday 16th May. Ph. 52 1344.

what? — ✳ *LOST* ✳

where? — "Bluey" is a small black Kelpie dog (6 months old). She's wearing a collar but no tags. We lost her in the Cheltenham area on

when? — Sunday 16th May. She's a family pet and missed by 3 children.

who? — If you find her please phone 52 1344.

Exercise 8

Choose one of the situations below and write the advertisement required. Make rough drafts first. If you wish, work with another student.

a) You are moving house. You want to sell a number of items of furniture before you move. You decide to have a garage sale. You write a classified advertisement.

b) You are having a party for your son's or daughter's 18th birthday. You need some help with the cooking and serving of the food. You write a classified advertisement to find someone.

c) For your next holiday, you are planning to drive from your town or city to somewhere else in Australia. You would like company and someone to share the driving. You write an advertisement to put on a notice-board at work or school.

d) You and some friends want to form a band. You need a guitarist who can play your kind of music. You write an advertisement to put in the window of the local record shop.

e) You are starting up a business (e.g. window cleaning, lawn mowing, secretarial services, photography) and you want to attract customers. You write a classified advertisement to put in the local newspaper.

Exercise 9

Do you need to write an advertisement? Write it now.

COMMON ABBREVIATIONS

EMPLOYMENT

exp.	experience	p.a.	per annum
f.t.	full-time	p.t.	part-time
h.p.w.	hours per week	qual.	qualified
hrs/day	hours per day	sal.	salary
Mon–Fri	Monday to Friday	wgs	wages
neg.	negotiable		

ACCOMMODATION

avail.	available	nr	near
b.r.	bedroom	pos.	position
cl.	close	p.w.	per week
cpts	carpets	refs	references
dble	double	rm	room
fem. (f)	female	s.c.	self-contained
f.furn.	fully furnished	sngl.	single
gar.	garage	spce	space
gdn	garden	stn	station
grnd fl.	ground floor	trans.	transport
l.u.g.	lock up garage	unf.	unfurnished
m.	male	wk	week
mod.	modern		

GENERAL

aft.	after	lge	large
a.h.	after hours	mths	months
br. new	brand new	no.	number
col.	colour	o.n.o.	or near(est) offer
cond.	condition	ph.	phone
exc.	excellent	tel.	telephone
gd	good	yrs	years

9 Personal letters

Introduction

Personal letters usually have one or more of the following purposes:
- to thank
- to send greetings or express your feelings about some occasion or event
- to apologize
- to invite
- to make arrangements
- to make or renew contact with someone
- to give news
- to request news
- to accompany enclosed material (photos, gifts, etc.)
- to reply to another letter.

Read the letter below and discuss which of the purposes above are covered. (Are some purposes more important than others? How do you know?)

---

107 Smith St.
A beautiful sunny 19ᵗʰ of November.

Dear Diane,

At last I've found a quiet moment (Sally snores away upstairs) to write and enclose some photos and to say thank you for the fantastic jumper. It looks great – all my friends want one just like it!

Life goes on at 107 – much the same as when you left. My work is now finished and so I find I never know what to do with myself in Sally's sleep times – will I sew, garden, write letters, do my tax (boring!), clean the house (more boring!) etc etc. Of course, Sally is usually awake before I've done anything.

Guess what – I've become involved in local politics – can you believe it – ME? It's to do with high-rise buildings in the suburb. Unfortunately, the meetings start at 9.30 pm (yawn). If I stay awake they're very interesting.

Bruce has taken up judo! We try not to laugh when he gets into his "pyjamas" (as Sally calls them). Anyway, he loves it.

Ah. There's Sally – must go. Look forward to seeing you on the long weekend in January. Hope all is well. Thanks again for the jumper.

Love Sarah x

P.S. The photos were taken in September at the lake.

Now read these points and discuss the questions:

i) Write your address and the date in the top right-hand corner. This is often done informally, and sometimes the address is not necessary at all.

How is the date unusual here?

ii) Begin your letter with a greeting of some kind. 'Dear . . . ' is by far the most common.

What other ways have you seen?

iii) Use the first paragraph to set the scene and to state the main purpose of your letter (if there is one). If replying to a letter, say thank you for it here.

How does the writer of this letter set the scene? What purposes does she mention?

iv) Organize the rest of your letter into paragraphs. In general, you should begin a new paragraph every time you change topics but this may not be necessary in a short letter.

What is the topic of each paragraph in this letter?

v) Don't worry too much about punctuation rules.

  – You can often use a dash (–) instead of a full stop or a comma or even a question mark.
  – You can use exclamation marks, capital letters and underlining to add emphasis.
  – You can use brackets to separate anything extra to the main thoughts.

Note the use of these features in the letter.

vi) Use the last paragraph to send good wishes, say goodbyes, mention future meetings and so on. It is common to begin this paragraph with a reason for ending the letter (time to go to bed, to the post office, etc.).

What reason for ending is given here?

vii) Finish your letter with a farewell message of some kind. Common endings are:

love   *see you soon*
all my love   *best wishes*
love and kisses   *regards*
bye for now

What other endings have you seen?

viii) Add anything you have forgotten to say as a postscript (PS). You sometimes see more than one postscript to a letter (PPS, PPPS, and so on).

Where does the information in this PS belong?

Exercise 1

Sometimes you need to write very short letters which have only one purpose.
– Decide what is the purpose of these letters. (Use the list in the Introduction.)
– Study the underlined words. They will be useful in your own letters.

a)

Dear Chris,   12 June, 1988

Thank you so much for your hospitality and kindness last weekend. It was very kind of you to give me a bed at such short notice. I hope I can repay you in the same way some time.

Regards,
Nick.

b)

2 Short St,
New Town
6/6/87.

Dear Mary and family,

I was very sad to hear about your mother's sudden death. Please accept my deepest sympathy. I only met her briefly, but remember her as a warm and generous person.

I am sorry I was unable to come down for the funeral. If there is any way I can help out, please let me know.

Yours sincerely

Graeme.

c)

12.7.87

Dear Anna,

Just a short note to let you know that I won't be able to meet you at the station. I've arranged for a taxi to be there at 12 noon. If it doesn't arrive – don't panic! Ring Tim at work (67023) and he can arrange something. Sorry about all this. See you soon.

Love F.

71

d)

> 60 Stacey St,
> Banksia
> 6/5/88
>
> Dear Mr and Mrs Price,
>
> Hello. I'm writing to introduce myself. My name is Katherine Peters, and I'm staying in Australia for about 6 months. I'm a friend of Mark's and he told me to look you up. I'll be in Brisbane on the 24th and I wondered if you'd mind if I called in. I shall ring first. I hope this doesn't inconvenience you at all, as I'm looking forward to meeting you both.
>
> Best wishes,
> K. Peters

e)

> 26th Feb.
>
> Dear Erica & Jo,
> We just heard the news! Congratulations on the birth of Joanna. We're all delighted. Glad to hear that everything went well and that you're back at home already. I will send something suitable soon. Till then – take care of yourselves and of Joanna, of course.
>
> Much love,
> Anne & Chris x

Exercise 2

This paragraph from a personal letter needs punctuation.
– Read it first for general meaning.
– Read it again, this time thinking about the missing punctuation.
– Now rewrite it, putting in punctuation to make its meaning clear.

perhaps gail has told you about the new man in my life paul schleger sometimes i cant quite believe that there is really someone in the world like him of course the problem is that hes in sydney maybe moving back to brisbane while im in brisbane now but moving to perth why is love always so difficult

Exercise 3

a) Questions are common in personal letters. Sometimes you might give news of your own and then ask your reader a related question.
   e.g.

> I'm learning to type.
> I thought it might improve
> my job chances. By the way,
> are you still doing your
> carpentry course?

Below are five extracts from personal letters. They have been divided into two parts. Match the parts on the left (news) with parts on the right (related questions).

i)   *Well, I've finally done it — I've got my licence. I was sick of everyone nagging me.*

A   *Have you been back lately? Lots of changes. You wouldn't recognize Xavier St.*

ii) *The big news is — I'm in love! I'm the happiest I've ever been.*

B   *How was yours? I bet you can't beat that for excitement!*

iii) *Gina is now at school. She loves it — thank goodness!*

C   *How about you? Have you changed your mind about it? I remember how you hated the lessons.*

iv) *I've just returned from a weekend in Perth — had a great time catching up on all the news.*

D   *Has William started yet or is he still only 4 (I've forgotten)?*

v)   *Xmas was exciting in Tower St this year. We had a baby born in the next door flat on Xmas Eve, a surprise overseas visitor for Xmas dinner, and then, on Boxing Day, the dog had 6 pups!*

E   *Which reminds me, how's Mauro? Are you still together?*

⟫→

b) Sometimes you might keep all your questions about your reader until the last paragraph of your letter. Look at this writer's last paragraph.

> Well, That's it for now. What's new with you? Do write — I'm starved of news from home. What's happening with your job? You talked of leaving — have you? What's Joseph up to? Jack? Bruno? I haven't head from them in ages. How's Melbourne? I miss it, you know. Anyway, till next time.
>
> Michael

- Think of someone you would like to write to at the moment.
- Think of the areas of his or her life that you would like to know something about (sport, study, family, other friends, etc.).
- Write a paragraph asking questions about these areas. Use one of the following to begin your paragraph.

Well, I must stop now. What's your news?

That's all the news from this end. What about you?

No more news to tell. Write soon and tell me yours.

Anyway — I must finish now. What's happening in your life?

Note: You might be able to use this paragraph in a later exercise.

Exercise 4

a) The letter below is a reply to another letter. Find and write out the parts that tell you this. These will be helpful to you in (b) and in exercises 7 and 8.

> *Dear Ella,*
>   *As usual, I've taken months to reply — SORRY! It was great to hear from you at Christmas — hope you had a good one. I stayed with Kim and Mike again at Murray Bridge — lots of swimming, fishing, lazing about in the sun and so on.*
>   *All that seems a long time ago now — I've been working for 6 weeks. I really enjoy it — though it's <u>very very</u> busy. Glad to hear you've got some part-time work — how's it going?*

> *What great news! You may be back here at the end of the year. I'll keep on the lookout for jobs — would you like me to send you some advertisements?*
>   *Pleased to hear that Katy is her old self. I must write to her soon.*
>   *Must stop now — I'm at work and have lots to do.*
>   *Write soon,*
>   *Vin*
>
> *P.S. Thanks for those newspaper clippings — they were <u>very</u> interesting.*
>
> *P.P.S. You mentioned Tim Payne — what a surprise him leaving like that — had any news lately?*

b) Sometimes you might begin a letter of reply by referring to *all* the news contained in the letter you received. Look at this writer's first paragraph.

> *Dear Rosa,*
>   *Thank you for your long, long letter. What a lot of news you had to tell! Congratulations on your terrific pass — well done! But what's this about stopping work? I was shocked — think carefully about it, won't you? Great news about K.M. — I look forward to seeing her.*

Look again at the letter in the Introduction. Imagine that you are Diane and that you are replying to that letter.
- Note down the points you will mention in your letter.
- Draft the first paragraph, referring to all those points (ask questions, make comments, express gladness, etc.).
- Revise your paragraph as needed.

Exercise 5

a) Think of someone you know well. Draft a paragraph about that person which would be of interest to another friend who has not seen him or her for a long time. Mention, for example, work, study, hobbies, relationships, health and so on.

— Begin by brainstorming (see Unit 1, *Preparing to write*).
— Revise your draft as needed.

Note: You might be able to use this paragraph in a later exercise.

b) Read the newspaper article below. Imagine that the event it reports happened near your house and that you saw part of it happen. Draft a paragraph about it which could be included in a letter to someone you know.

— Begin by noting down the points you will mention. The underlined parts will help you.
— Revise your draft as needed.
— Compare your paragraph with those of other students.

Note: You might be able to use this paragraph in a later exercise.

Once robbed, twice shy, so she ran

By TERESA MANNIX

Mrs Moyra Britten was tied up and robbed at knifepoint at the Downer Post Office three years ago. When the same thing looked like happening yesterday, she didn't hang around.

"I ran out the door yelling like a banshee," she said.

The robber, with a handkerchief over his mouth and a black plastic gun which Mrs Britten did not notice, barely had time to order her to stay in the office section before she took off.

The culprit, who managed to elude police after an extended chase at about 10.30am yesterday, escaped with what she estimated to be about $100.

A worker at a nearby Playoust construction site, Mr Lex Boyd, took up the story.

"I heard a woman screaming for help and saw a bloke running out of the post office carrying a bag," he said. "I chased him, but he had too much of a head start."

The thief dropped the gun as he raced through the grounds of the Downer Infants and Primary School, vaulted over a fence and disappeared behind some houses in Bradfield Street.

Mr Boyd and his two workmates who helped in the chase said the police had arrived on the scene within a remarkably short time.

But they failed to apprehend the man after extensive searches of the area.

The Identikit picture of the man police are seeking after a robbery at the Downer Post Office yesterday.

Police are seeking a clean-shaven man with neat, dark hair, about 1.7 metres tall, last seen wearing a blue-knitted jumper and blue denim jeans.

Exercise 6

a) Organizing your thoughts into paragraphs helps your reader to understand your meaning.
   - Think of someone you would like to write to and who you have not seen for a long time.
   - Write down about five areas of activity in your life which would be of interest to this person (work, study, family, etc.).
   - Use these areas as topic headings. Underneath each, write down related events, comments, questions and so on.
     e.g.

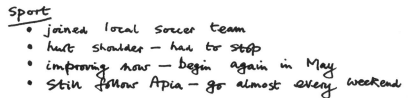

   - Choose one area to write into a paragraph.
   - Begin by reordering your notes if necessary.
   - Revise as needed.

b) If you wish, continue with the letter above, using your notes to write more paragraphs.
   - Write a beginning and an ending for your letter. (Other letter samples in the unit will help you.)
   - Send your letter!

Exercise 7

Choose two or three of the situations below and write the letters. Make them realistic by including personal details of your current activities.

a) You have just received some photos from a friend who visited you last month. You write a letter of thanks and tell your friend briefly what has happened in your life since then.
b) You have just heard that a friend is getting married. You write a letter of congratulations and tell him or her some news.
c) Years ago you met and travelled with a person from another country. Suddenly you receive a letter from this friend, telling you that he or she is coming to live in Australia. You write a letter back and include some advice for your friend's first days in the country.
d) You have just moved from another city. You are missing some close friends you had there. You write a letter telling them how you feel and describing your first few weeks in your new city.
e) You are planning a trip to another part of the country. You write to some friends who live there, telling them of the trip and expressing your wish to see them.
f) You receive a letter from your parents telling you about a friend's sickness. You write to the friend and include some news of your family and of your activities.

g) It is a friend's birthday. You send your birthday wishes in a letter which includes your news of the past year.

h) A family member has gone to live overseas for a year. He or she has been gone for four months now and you have not had a letter. You are rather annoyed and so you write a letter.

i) Some friends have written to invite you to spend the holidays with them. You write back expressing your thanks and telling them whether or not you can go.

j) Someone has sent you a gift for your birthday. You write a letter of thanks and tell them about your birthday celebration.

Exercise 8

Is there a personal letter you need to write at the moment? If so, write it now!

10 Formal letters

Introduction

Do you ever get formal letters from, or do you have to write to:

local councils	government departments
banks	education bodies
insurance companies	solicitors
landlords or rental agents	travel or holiday companies
gas or electricity bodies	others?

Keep copies of such letters. They will be useful in many of the exercises in this unit.

Look at the two letters below. One (Letter A) is a formal letter to a bank manager. The other (Letter B) is a personal letter to a friend.

LETTER A

11 Hopetown Rd
Mitcham
8/12/88

The Manager
Federal Bank
10 Hunter St
Mitcham :

Dear Sir / Madam,
Re: Account No. 178856A
I am writing to notify you of a change of address for the above account in my name.
The previous address was 299 Miller St, North Mitcham. The new address is that shown above.

Thanking you for your assistance.

Yours sincerely,

T Adoni
(Mrs) T. Adoni

LETTER B

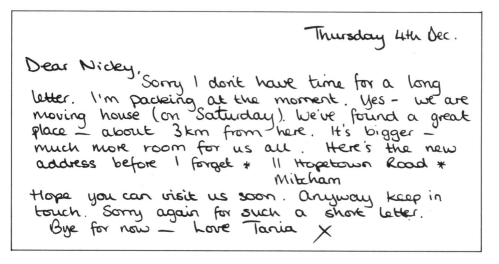

Thursday 4th Dec.

Dear Nicky,
Sorry I don't have time for a long letter. I'm packing at the moment. Yes - we are moving house (on Saturday). We've found a great place — about 3 km from here. It's bigger — much more room for us all. Here's the new address before I forget * 11 Hopetown Road * Mitcham
Hope you can visit us soon. Anyway keep in touch. Sorry again for such a short letter.
Bye for now — Love Tania X

Work in groups of two or three. Discuss:
— What is the common purpose of the letters?
— How is the formal letter different from the personal letter? (Think about, for example, its general appearance, layout, content and the words and expressions used in it.)
— Why are they different?
Compare your findings with those of other groups.

When writing a formal letter:

iii) Write the name, the position and the address of the person you are writing to here (lower than your address). ———

    You will not always know the name or the position. Use what you know.

iv) Use:
   — The person's surname (Dear Mrs Smith) if you know it. Only use the first name if you know him or her very well.
   — 'Dear Sir' if you are writing to a man and don't know his name.
   — 'Dear Madam' if you are writing to a woman and don't know her name.
   — 'Dear Sir/Madam' or 'Dear Sir or Madam' if you don't know the name or the sex. You can also use the person's position (Dear Councillor/Resident/Manager/etc.).

LETTER A

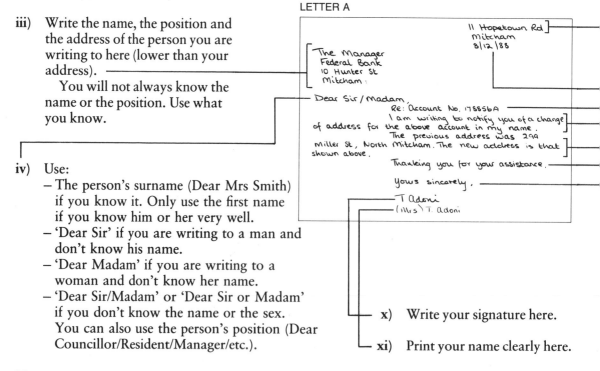

11 Hopetown Rd
Mitcham
8/12/88

The Manager
Federal Bank
10 Hunter St
Mitcham :

Dear Sir / Madam,
    Re: Account No. 178856A
    I am writing to notify you of a change of address for the above account in my name.
    The previous address was 299 Miller St, North Mitcham. The new address is that shown above.

    Thanking you for your assistance.

    Yours sincerely,

    T Adoni
    (Mrs) T. Adoni

x) Write your signature here.

xi) Print your name clearly here.

i)   Write your address here.

ii)   Write the date here. You can write it in many ways:
Dec 8, 1988   8 Dec, 1988   8/12/88
Dec 8th, 1988   8th Dec, 1988   8.12.88
(88 is acceptable for 1988)

v)   You can write a short statement here to introduce the main point of your letter. ('Re' means 'about'.) This is not always necessary.

vi)   Begin with a sentence which explains the purpose of the letter. (You should do this even if you write a statement as in (v).) If you are writing in reply, mention the date of the letter received and any reference code. (See letter C in exercise 1.)

vii)   Then write any extra information. Keep to the point. Only mention what is necessary.
   If the letter is very short you could put everything in one paragraph. If it is longer and includes several points, you will need more than one paragraph.

viii)   End with a sentence like this. You will see other examples in the letters in this unit.

ix)   Follow these rules for endings:
– Use 'Yours faithfully' where you have used 'Dear Sir' or 'Dear Madam'.
– Use 'Yours sincerely' where you have used the person's name ('Dear Mrs Smith').
'Yours sincerely' is, however, seen more and more in both cases.
   You can use 'Best wishes', 'Regards', 'Kind regards', etc. in letters which are not very formal and where you know the person or have spoken to them often on the phone.

xii)   Write clearly and neatly. Don't cross out.

<u>*Exercise 1*</u>

You have received this letter:

LETTER C

H.H.D. Insurance

HILTON HOUSE   300 PITT ST   SYDNEY 2000

In reply please quote: JC:RD   6th Jan, 1988

....

....

....

Dear .... ,

I wish to remind you that payment on your Household
Contents Insurance policy fell due on 1/1/88. $59.10
is now owing. I shall be pleased to receive your
cheque in settlement at your earliest convenience.

Yours sincerely

R Douglas

Ms R. Douglas
Supervisor

Tel: 22 2553/22 2554
Telegraphic address: HINSU

You have decided to cancel your policy and have written a letter to the insurance
company to tell them so. Below is the body of your letter.
— Set it out correctly.
— Punctuate it. (See Unit 5, *Punctuation*, for help.)
— Address it correctly, using information from the letter above.
— Use your own name and address as sender and use today's date.

LETTER D

```
dear ms douglas i refer to your letter
(JC:RD) dated 6th january 1988 i wish to
advise you that i have decided to cancel my
household contents insurance policy i would
be grateful if you would acknowledge
receipt of my letter yours sincerely
```

Exercise 2

a) The opening sentence of a formal letter usually tells you the purpose of the letter. Below are four examples. Match them to the incomplete letters (E,F,G,H) which follow.

i)   I would like some information on the courses you offer at your college.

ii) Please find enclosed a cheque for $65.00.

iii) I refer to your letter dated 30/3/87, your reference number H6794.

iv) I am writing to inform you of an apparent error in your records.

LETTER E

....

This is to cover the enrolment fees for the weekend workshop on self-hypnosis (Aug.7th to 9th). Please forward a receipt to the above address.

LETTER F

....

It seems you have my address as 6/8 Downing St, Kensington. My correct address is 8/6 Downing St. Consequently correspondence from you has been delivered to my neighbour's house.
     Thank you for your cooperation in correcting this detail.

LETTER G

....

My interest is in computers. I have done two beginner courses in the subject and now wish to attempt a more advanced course. Could you please send me any brochures that you have available, including details of cost and enrolment procedures?
     Thank you for your assistance in this matter.

LETTER H

....

You stated that I would shortly receive a refund of $45 for over-payment of student union fees. Six weeks have now passed and I have not received anything from you. Could you please look into the matter? I would appreciate prompt action.

b) Make up your own opening sentences to complete the letters below. Begin by reading each letter carefully and deciding what the main purpose is.

LETTER I

....

I am moving to Melbourne in early May and will be needing full-time care for both my 4-year-old and 2-year-old. As far as I know we will be living in the inner western suburbs so I am particularly interested to know what is available there.
     I would be grateful to receive any information you have as soon as possible.

LETTER J

....

You said that there were three books overdue. I feel there must be some mistake as I am absolutely sure that I have returned both "Kissing: A hundred years" and "The Dark, Dark Night". I do still have "Born To Be King" and apologize for not returning it before I moved interstate. It is enclosed here.
     Please check your records again. I hope this will be the end of the matter.

Exercise 3

Formal letters often contain words or expressions that are not common in everyday speech. For example, in Letter A above, the writer uses the expression 'notify you' where we would more commonly say 'tell you' or 'let you know'.

It is important to understand these expressions, but it is not always necessary to use them yourself. Sometimes your meaning will be clearer using words you know well.

The words and phrases on the left are taken from previous letters in this unit. Find each one in the letter indicated. Then match them with the more common expressions on the right.

Letter A
a) previous

b) assistance

Letter C

c) in settlement

d) at your earliest convenience

Letter D

e) advise

f) cancel

g) grateful

h) acknowledge receipt

Letter E

i) forward

Letter F

j) correspondence

k) cooperation

Letter H

l) stated

m) refund

n) prompt

Letter J

o) enclosed

1 thankful

2 in payment

3 send

4 said, wrote

5 stop, end

6 help

7 money paid back

8 let me know you have received

9 quick

10 included in the envelope

11 the one before

12 tell, inform

13 as soon as possible

14 help

15 letters

Exercise 4

Three sentences have been left out of the following letter. The sentences are given below. Rewrite the letter putting the sentences back in appropriate places.

LETTER K

Dear Mr Anderson,

                  I am writing to give you one month's notice of my intention to vacate the flat at 1/35 Barker Rd, Malvern. The increase in the rent means that I can no longer afford to live here. So should you have any flats available nearby that are less expensive, I would be grateful if you would contact me. In the meantime, I have no objection to your showing people through the flat.

                  Thanking you for your assistance.

                  Yours sincerely,

---

i)   My home number is 519 4073 or I can be contacted at work on 211 4416.

ii)   However, I do ask that you give me at least one day's notice so that I can be sure that the flat is tidy.

iii) I would, however, like to continue renting in this area.

Exercise 5

Arrange the parts below to make a complete letter.

LETTER L

i)   I am interested in Package D (the 20 day trek in Nepal).

ii)   Yours faithfully,

iii)   We look forward to your confirmation of our booking as soon as possible.

iv)   Thank you for the information you sent about Himalayan Expedition Holidays.

v)   We would prefer the Sept. 20th departure date, with a second choice of Oct. 15th.

vi)   I would like to make a definite booking for two people.

vii)   Dear Sir/Madam,

viii) Himalayan Expedition Holidays,
      88 Queen St,
      Perth

Exercise 6

Choose from the linking words provided below to fill the spaces in the following letter.

LETTER M

Mrs D. Paul,
Principal

Dear Mrs Paul,
            I am writing to inform you that we are about to
move out of the area (i) .... that my daughter,
Alice, will (ii) .... be leaving school on Sept
18th.
            I have already contacted her new school and made
arrangements for her to begin in a month. They would,
(iii) ...., like to have copies of her recent school
reports. In the confusion of packing I have been unable to find
them, (iv) .... would it be possible for you to send
copies of them home with Alice.
            If there if anything else you would like to discuss,
please don't hesitate to contact me.
            Yours sincerely,

---

i)   and, also, because, so
ii) so, therefore, because
iii) although, so, therefore, however
iv) and, so, because, but

Exercise 7

Short formal notes to explain your own or a family member's absence from work or school are sometimes necessary. They can be set out as a note, e.g.

6/9/88

Dear Mr. Jackson,
        Please excuse Tim from school next
week as he has to spend one week in
hospital to have an operation on his foot.
                                    Mr. Nick Pavlos.

or as a formal letter.
e.g.

---

12 Boronia St
Claremont

17th Oct, 1987

Dear Ms Farnham,
    I am writing to inform you that I will be absent from work until Monday, 24th October, because of an accident in which I broke my ankle.
    Should you need to contact me, I will be available on 331 7722.

Yours sincerely,

Lyn Taylor

In both, the language is usually formal and only the main point is mentioned. Complete these formal notes, using the cue words provided.

i) *Dear Mrs Deloso,*

    I am sorry that I was unable to attend...

....

....

(appointment, Monday; another appointment, next Monday)

ii) *Dear Mr Nyland,*

    Connie was absent from school...

....

....

(five days, flu, copy of doctor's certificate)

iii) *Dear Miss Phillips,*

    Miguel was not at school ....

....

....

(this morning, dentist, again next Tuesday morning)

Exercise 8

Look through all the formal letters in this unit. Write down the last sentence from each. Make sure you understand what they mean. Keep them to help you in exercises 9 and 10, and in your own formal letter writing.

Exercise 9

The list below contains some useful words that often occur in formal letters. Related words have been grouped together. This can help you memorize spellings.
– Learn to spell these words using the techniques outlined in Unit 4, *Spelling*.
– Add any other words you think might be useful (adding them to the groups where possible).

sincerely	advise	thankful
faithfully	advice	grateful
received	enclosed	appreciate
receipt	attached	
request	application	notify
refer	information	
refund	cooperation	correct

Exercise 10

Choose a holiday that interests you from the advertisements below.

HOUSEBOAT HOLIDAYS

Fully self-contained, 6 berth houseboats.

An inexpensive and relaxing holiday for you and your friends or family on the beautiful Murray River at Renmark.

Enquiries: "Houseboat Holidays" P.O. Box 206 Renmark, S.A. 5341.

TRAVEL DIARY

FRENCH ADVENTURE. 35 day tour of France from $6490 departing 4th September.
CATHEDRALS OF EUROPE. 24 day tour of Italy, France, U.K., from $5175 departing 9th September.
NEW ZEALAND EXPLORER. 18 day coach tour from $2012 departing 12th September.
SPAIN, FRANCE, ITALY, PORTUGAL (Fatima). Christian tour group departing 16th September. 30 days from $4985.
JAPAN AND NAGOYA FESTIVAL. 15 day tour of Japan. 15 days from $3680 departing 5th October.
CULTURAL TOUR OF EUROPE. Great performances, great cities. 26 days from $7375 departing 9th October.
JOURNEY OF A LIFETIME. Luxury hotel barge cruise through Europe. 42 days from $6050 departing 22nd October.
Check your travel diary now with

Penthouse Travel (A.J.C.)

5th Floor, 28 O'Connell Street, SYDNEY
Phone (02) 231-1155, toll-free: (008) 22-1369
Telex: AA73192. Licence No. B. 1853

- Use some of the ideas suggested in Unit 1, *Preparing to write*, to make notes about further information you would like, and necessary personal details you would have to give.
- Draft a letter, using the ideas in Unit 2, *Drafting*, to help you.
- Revise your draft. Check that:
  - your opening sentence explains the purpose of your letter
  - you have included all necessary information
  - your spelling, layout and punctuation are correct
  - your copy is neat.
  Refer to Unit 3, *Revising*.

Exercise 11

Choose one or more of the situations below and write an appropriate letter.

a) You are about to move house. You write to the bank, telling them your new address. (Use the name and address of your own bank.)

b) You write to your local real estate agent outlining a number of repairs that need to be done to your flat or house. (Use the name and address of your agent if you have one. Otherwise use: Mr Bartlett, Bartlett and Peterson Real Estate, 25 Stanley Ave, Brompton.)

c) On telephoning your insurance company to cancel an insurance policy, you are told, 'Please put it in writing'. You write the necessary letter. (Use your own policy number and insurance company if you have one. Otherwise use: Policy No.: H239275; name and address: Security Insurance, 82 Maxwell St, Melbourne, 3000).

d) You write a letter to your local council, thanking them for the fine work they have done in establishing a park in your suburb and suggesting one or two other projects which might improve things for local residents. (If possible find the address of your local council in the telephone directory. Otherwise address your letter to: Brighton Municipal Council, Town Hall, Brighton.)

e) You are interested in one of the correspondence courses advertised below.
You write away to enrol on the course or to ask for the course guide.

The Adult Education by Correspondence School

In 1989 we are offering courses in:

- Australian history
- Basic carpentry
- Bookkeeping
- Computer programming
- Dressmaking
- Fashion design
- Hairdressing
- Home renovating
- Japanese cooking
- Picture framing
  and more.

Enrol **now,** enclosing a cheque or money order for $65,
or send for our comprehensive course guide.

The Adult Education by Correspondence School
P.O. Box 727 Paddington 2010
Tel. 332 5539

f) You write a letter in response to one of the following advertisements.

Exercise 12

Follow the steps outlined in exercise 10 above to write a formal letter that *you* need to write at the moment.

11 *Job applications*

Introduction

When you apply for a job, you may have to:
— write a letter of application
— fill in an application form
— write a résumé of your background and experience. (A résumé is also called
   a Curriculum Vitae.)
Your application may be used to decide if you get an interview for a job, so it
is very important to give the right impression.

   Below are two letters of application. They were written in response to the job
advertisement shown. Each letter was attached to a résumé. (For an example of
a résumé see exercise 3 in this unit.)
— Compare the two applications.
— Discuss which gives the better impression and why.

TENNIS COACH
We are looking for an experienced and qualified
person to fill a vacancy for a full-time tennis coach.
Duties include individual and group tuition of both
children and adults.
Apply in writing to:
The Tennis Centre, Station St, Marrickville

LETTER A
Dear Sir/Madam,
   I would like to apply for the position of full-time tennis
coach, advertised in the January edition of "Sports Monthly".
   I feel I am well qualified for the position. I have a Level
2 coaching certificate and I have had two years experience as
a part-time tennis coach with Murrays Tennis School. I am an
enthusiastic and friendly person and I enjoy working with
people, both young and old.
   A position with your club would give me the opportunity to
work full-time in the job that I love, and to work with both
children and adults.
   A resume giving details of my qualifications and experience
is attached.
   I would be happy to attend an interview at any time
convenient to you.
   Yours sincerely,

LETTER B

Dear Sir/Madam,

    I noticed that you are looking for someone to work as a tennis coach. I would really like to do that. I'm pretty good at tennis. I am working at the moment as a cook but I don't like that much. I'd rather play tennis all day. Before this job I used to work as a kitchen hand in a restaurant. At the moment I'm living in Newtown so this job would be really convenient for me. I wouldn't have to travel far to work.

    I hope to hear from you soon.

Yours sincerely,

When writing job application letters to accompany a résumé:

i)   Mention the position you are applying for and where you learnt of the vacancy.

ii) Expand on some points about your background or experience, showing how they are relevant to this job. Do not repeat all the information on your resume or application form.

iii) Emphasize your interest in and suitability for the job. If possible, show you have some knowledge of what the company does.

iv) Mention that you have attached a copy of your resume or a completed application form.

v) State that you are willing to attend an interview.

vi) Set your letter out clearly. Follow closely the layout and punctuation of formal letters (see Unit 11). If possible, have your letter typed. If not, make sure it is very neatly written.

vii) Keep a copy of the letter and the advertisement.

Points (i) to (v) above correspond to parts of Letter A above. Find those parts in the letter.

Exercise 1

GARDENER
temporary, part-time.

We have a temporary vacancy for a gardener to work on a part-time basis (15 hours/wk) for a period of approx. 12 months. Experience in the care of Australian native plants is desirable. Weekend work is involved. Salary $180 per week.
Please apply in writing to
Mr J. Malloy, P.O. Box 212, Chesterfield 2054.
Applications close 1st April.

Below is a draft of an application letter for the job advertised above. Rewrite the letter.

– Add the necessary punctuation. (Refer to Unit 5, *Punctuation*, if you need to.)

– Organize it into paragraphs, using the same pattern as in Letter A above.

⋙→

These cue words will help:
i)   position/vacancy
ii) qualifications/experience/suitability
iii) why this job/company?
iv) résumé
v)   contact/interview

Dear Sir/Madam
i am particularly interested in applying for the part-time
position of gardener advertised in the daily planet on
march 14th i am a keen horticulturist and am at present in
the final year of a 3 year part-time course at rosebank
technical college i am specializing in the area of
australian native plants the position you offer would
therefore be ideal for me it would allow me to continue my
studies and to work in an area where i can apply my
specialist knowledge i have attached a resume outlining my
qualifications and experience please contact me any time to
arrange for an interview yours sincerely

Exercise 2

Read the following job advertisement. Discuss the qualifications and experience that an applicant might mention in a letter.

Complete the job application letter below.

SALES/STORE PERSON

Opportunity for full-time position in large scale Discount Retail Store.

Duties include; Counter sales, store work, heavy lifting. Driver's licence for deliveries.

Must be neat, reliable, willing to work hard. Ability to speak Italian an advantage. Award rates.

Apply in writing to:
**THE MANAGER
P.O. BOX 60,
COWAN**

Dear .... ,
            I am writing to apply ....
....
....
            I have worked as ....
....
....
....
            I am..
....
and I consider myself a most suitable
applicant for the job.
            I have enclosed...........................
....
            Please contact me..........................
....
            Yours sincerely,

Exercise 3

A résumé is a summary of your personal information and experience. It is important to present it very clearly. Look at the example below.

```
PERSONAL          NAME:             Augusta Neves
                  ADDRESS:          3 The Parade, Stanmore, 2048
                  TELEPHONE NUMBER: (02) 560 1126
                  DATE OF BIRTH:    17th March, 1966

EDUCATION         1972 - 82 Primary and Secondary school,
                            Santiago, Chile
                  1983      School Certificate, Ashfield High School
                            Subjects: English, Maths, Commerce,
                                    Spanish, Geography

WORK EXPERIENCE   1987 -  * Sales assistant, Morris Bros., City
                            Store, Book Dept
                            Duties: Customer service, ordering,
                            book displays
                  1985 - 86 Sales assistant, Burrows Pharmacy,
                            Stanmore
                            Duties: Customer service, advice on
                            cosmetics
                  1984 - 85 Waitress, Francesca's Restaurant,
                            Campsie

OTHER INFORMATION Typing: 50 wpm
                  Languages: fluent in Spanish and Italian
                  Hobbies: swimming, basketball, reading

REFEREES        * P. Botham (Manager),
                  Morris Bros., City Store, Book Dept,
                  Elizabeth St, Sydney 2000
                  271 4435

                  Dr T. Angelis,
                  Burrows Pharmacy,
                  39 Crystal St, Stanmore 2048
                  560 4459
```

Notes:

1 For work experience, put your most recent job first, then list other jobs going back in time. If a past job was relevant to this one, mention the duties you were responsible for. Work experience programs and voluntary work can also be mentioned.

2 For referees, write the name and address of two people who you know well. At least one should be a work reference. Check first with the people you name.

Write your own résumé.

– Use the example and the notes above as a guide.
– Write as many drafts as you need to get it correct.
– Ask your teacher to check it for you.
– Type it if possible and make copies to keep.

Exercise 4

For some jobs you may need to fill out a job application form. This will replace your résumé.

Collect two or three job application forms like the one below. Fill them out for practice.
— Print answers clearly. Use block letters if required (e.g. ITALIAN).
— Write N/A (not applicable) in the space, if a question is not relevant to you.
— Use note form, not full sentences, to give details.

APPLICATION FOR EMPLOYMENT

POSITION APPLIED: _____ 2nd Choice: _____

TYPE OF POSITION DESIRED: full time_____part time_____on call_____casual _____

TYPE OF WORK MOST QUALIFIED FOR: _____Salary Expected $ _____

AVAILABILITY TO COMMENCE: _____

WILL YOU WORK NIGHTS OR ON ROTATING SHIFT?   YES ☐   NO ☐

PERSONAL DETAILS

NAME: _____ _____ _____
SURNAME   OTHER NAMES   MAIDEN NAME (if applicable)

ADDRESS: _____ **Telephone:** Home _____
_____ Post Code _____ Business/Message _____

SEX: MALE ☐   FEMALE ☐   HEIGHT _____   WEIGHT _____

CAN YOU PRODUCE IDENTIFICATION: PASSPORT OR BIRTH CERTIFICATE?   YES ☐   NO ☐

DATE OF BIRTH: _____ TOWN AND COUNTRY OF BIRTH: _____

IF NOT AUSTRALIAN CITIZEN, DO YOU HAVE RESIDENCY STATUS: YES ☐   NO ☐

IF YES, SPECIFY TYPE: PERMANENT ☐ TEMPORARY ☐   DATE OF EXPIRY..................

MARITAL STATUS: MARRIED ☐   SINGLE ☐   DIVORCED ☐   WIDOWED ☐   SEPARATED ☐

NAME OF SPOUSE: _____ OCCUPATION _____

CHILDREN: _____
(fill in year of birth of)   M _____
F _____

EDUCATION	NAME & ADDRESS OF SCHOOL	DURATION OF STUDIES		DEGREE/CERT OBTAINED	MAJOR COURSE OF STUDY
		From Mth Yr	To Mth Yr		
PRIMARY					
SECONDARY					
UNIVERSITY					
TECHNICAL/PROFESSIONAL					
OTHERS					

EMPLOYMENT RECORD (PRESENT OR LAST EMPLOYER FIRST)

COMPANY NAME AND ADDRESS	EMPLOYER'S BUSINESS	EMPLOYED FROM	TO	POSITION DUTIES	GROSS SALARY	REASON FOR LEAVING

SKILLS

TYPE	QUALIFICATION	PROFICIENCY	REMARKS (OTHER RELEVANT INFORMATION)

LANGUAGES

WHAT LANGUAGES DO YOU KNOW?	IS IT YOUR MOTHER TONGUE?	SPEAK GOOD	FAIR	POOR	WRITE GOOD	FAIR	POOR	UNDERSTAND GOOD	FAIR	POOR
	YES NO									

HOBBIES OR INTERESTS:

Exercise 5

The list below contains some words commonly used in job applications. They are arranged in groups to help you remember spellings. Use the techniques outlined in Unit 4, *Spelling*, to help you memorize these words.

preference
reference
experience

qualified
advertised
attached
pleased
experienced
interested

qualifications
information
position

enthusiastic
energetic

possible
responsible

advertisement
employment

company
opportunity
vacancy
ability
necessary

sincerely
extremely
recently
immediately
friendly

apply
reply

convenient
excellent

suitable
available

résumé

Exercise 6

The job application letter below is a canvassing letter, to enquire about the possibility of employment now or in the future. It was *not* written in response to an advertisement.

Find suitable words from the list in exercise 5 to complete the letter.

When you have chosen the words, try to write them from memory.

```
Dear Sir/Madam,
    I am writing to enquire about the possibility of (i) .............. .
I am (ii) .............. in any type of hotel or kitchen work.
    I have had three years (iii) .............. in the kitchen of a large
hotel in Perth. I was employed there as a kitchenhand but often
worked as an assistant chef.
    I (iv) .............. completed a special English course called
"English for Kitchenhands". It included a work experience program
one day per week, when I worked at the Mayfair Hotel.
    I would welcome an (v) .............. to work for the Hilton and I
feel I would make an (vi) .............. employee.
    I am (vii) .............. to start work (viii) .............. and am
willing to move if (ix) .............. .
    My (x) .............. and two (xi) .............. are attached.
    Should you have a (xii) .............. at present or foresee any in
the near future, I would be (xiii) .............. to hear from you.
    Yours sincerely,
```

Exercise 7

Find a job advertisement in the newspaper that is suitable for you, or use one of the examples below for practice.

CLEANER, 5 hrs, 9am – 2pm, Fri or Sat. $9 p.hr. Private home, Vaucluse. Please write enclosing copies of references: Box 301, GPO Sydney.

RECEPTIONIST Junior Casual for Doctors surgery 2 or 3 nights weekly, 5 – 7pm. Apply in own writing to Box 37 Rose Bay. 2029.

COUPLE

Must be familiar with sheep, property within 50 km from Adelaide in Barossa area. Good unfurnished accommodation, unsuit. for children. Good wages and conditions. References required.

Write to B16, Advertiser.

Seeking staff

The new Ryde Children's Centre, at 26 Flint Street, Nth Ryde, which will have 40 childcare places, is seeking about a dozen staff, including a trainee nurse and a casual kitchen helper. Applicants should write to the centre, to reach it no later than Monday, March 3. Further information can be obtained by telephoning Mrs Jill Lester on 881247.

ARTIST

Mosman Pk Art Studio requires Artist to do assembly, must also have the ability to draw and keen to learn airbrush illustration. Apply in writing to:
ALEX LAVERS
22 Waters Rd., Mosman Pk 6012.

YOUTH WORKER

Required for 20 weeks commencing late February. 3 days and 2 nights per week. Shift work. Applicants should be experienced in some area of youth work.
Car essential.
Applications in writing by Friday 24th January to The Chairperson, Newtown Youth Refuge, P.O. Box 579, Newtown 2042 Phone 516 2838.

MOTOR CYCLE MECHANIC

Clean neat person is required in our workshop. The successful applicant must be qualified and have an excellent working knowledge of Japanese motor cycles.
Applications in writing only addressed to:
The Manager
SOUTHERN MOTORS
444 South Road
Morphett Vale. 5162.

- Read your chosen advertisement several times.
- Underline important parts you should mention in your letter.
- Make some rough notes of the things you should mention.
- Write as many drafts as you need.
- If you intend to send your letter, ask someone to check it for you.

Exercise 8

If you are currently looking for work, think of a number of jobs you are interested in, and qualified to apply for.
- Find the names of several employers who might employ someone like you. (Use the Yellow Pages telephone directory, contacts you have or the experience of others in the class.)
- Prepare and draft a canvassing letter, asking if they have any vacancies. (Use the model in exercise 6 if necessary.)
- Revise carefully. Ask someone to check it.
- Type the letter and send it.

12 Letters of protest or complaint

Introduction

Have you ever written, or wanted to write, a letter to protest or complain about:
— a service (e.g. transport, post, telephone)
— something you bought (e.g. furniture, toys, household appliances)
— workmanship (e.g. building, painting, machine repairs)
— public facilities (e.g. parking, footpaths, roads)
— treatment you received (e.g. from shop assistants, government officials, parking officers)
— something else?
Writing a letter about these things can be a good way to 'let off steam', but the main aim is to get some action. What action did you want in the above cases?

Writing such a letter can take careful preparation, drafting and revising. Discuss the differences between these two letters. Which one is better? Why?

LETTER A

```
                           7/22 Downer Place
                           Downer. A.C.T.
                           14/7/88

Dear Sir/Madam,
              Look at these photos you
people developed! How can you expect people
to pay for the service you provide? I know
it wasn't my fault — everyone says I'm an
excellent photographer. I refuse to pay for
this rubbish. I won't stop at this, either.
The assistant I spoke to at the counter was
very rude as well. You should train your
staff to be more helpful and polite.

                      K. Bunt
                      K. Bunt
```

LETTER B

```
                                        6/2 Miller St,
                                        Watson. A.C.T.
                                        12/5/88

The Manager,
Kwikfilm Pty Ltd,
Stacey St,
Bankstown

Dear Sir/Madam,
    I am writing to complain about this set of photographs your
company developed recently.
    In my opinion, the photos are an awful colour and are not
worth the $12.45 that I paid for them.
    The film was new and my camera is a fairly expensive Canon
35mm, SLR manual. So, I don't think the quality of the prints
can be blamed on either the equipment or the film.
    I have enclosed the photos so you can have a look for
yourself.
    I would like the photos reprinted giving a better quality
colour, or otherwise a refund of the $12.45.
    I look forward to hearing from you at your earliest
convenience.
                    Yours faithfully,

                    J. Sonnenberg
                    J. Sonnenberg
```

Keep these points in mind when writing a letter of protest or complaint.

i)   Find out, before you write, who you should address your letter to.
ii)   Follow the layout and punctuation of formal letters (see Unit 10).
iii)   Arrange your points in paragraphs. (This may not be necessary in a very
       short letter.)
iv)   Say clearly what you are complaining about.
v)   Give exact details in a clear and ordered way.
vi)   Say clearly what action you expect or want.
vii)   Be polite, even if you are angry. Don't use insulting language or make
       personal attacks.
viii) Be business-like. Don't be chatty unless it is a short note to someone you
       know, for example, a neighbour (see examples in exercises 2 and 6).
ix)   Keep a copy of your letter. It may be important later to have a record of
       your complaint. You cannot have such a record if you complain in person
       or on the telephone.
x)   Sign off formally. 'Yours faithfully' or 'Yours sincerely' are best.

Exercise 1

a) Sometimes, you might need outside help in making a complaint. Many organizations (government and non-government) exist to provide this help.
   Find out, by using the telephone directory and/or making a telephone call, who you can write to if:
   i)   you have very noisy neighbours
   ii) your landlord or agent treats you unfairly
   iii) you have a problem with some goods or services you have paid for
   iv) an employer treats you unfairly because of your sex, age, nationality or marital status.

b) Ring up these organizations and ask them to send you information about your rights in these matters, and about the course of action you can take.

Exercise 2

a) The sentences below make up a short letter of complaint, written by one neighbour to another. However, the sentences are in the wrong order. Working with another student if possible, put them in the right order.

> *Dear Neighbour,*
>
> i)   *Could you try to do something about it?*
>
> ii) *And it's not the first time.*
>
> iii) *I don't like to be a pest, but one of your dogs (the little one) yelped for about 2 hours last night, from about 9 till 11.*
>
> iv) *I'd greatly appreciate it.*
>
> v)   *He often cries for hours when you are out.*
>
> vi) *He nearly drove me crazy!*
>
> vii) *I don't know what!*
>
>

Kay Chung
(upstairs)
>

b) Here are some sentences which make up a longer, more formal letter, written by a tenant to a rental agent. Put them in the right order. The underlined words will help you.

   Dear Mr Anders,
   i)   I <u>realize that</u> it's our responsibility as tenants to keep <u>it</u> clean and tidy, but this is impossible to do at present.
   ii) <u>I wish to complain about</u> the condition of the laundry in our building, 125 Baxter St, Darlinghurst.
   iii) <u>Secondly</u>, the door doesn't close properly, so leaves and other rubbish blow in.
   iv) Thanking you in anticipation of <u>that assistance</u>.
   v)   <u>Recently a further problem</u> has developed with pigeons nesting in the roof.
   vi) <u>Firstly</u>, the drain-pipe under the trough is leaking, and there is always a pool of water on the floor.

vii) I repeat that we are most willing to do our bit to keep it tidy, but we need your assistance too.

Yours sincerely,

L.J. Mitchell

Exercise 3

Choose the best wording for a formal letter of protest or complaint from each set of three below. Discuss why the one you choose is best.

a)
   i) My mother was staying with me last week and she tripped over a tree root and grazed her arm.
   ii) My mother was hurt last week when she tripped over a tree root outside my house.
   iii) Tree roots can trip people up, like they did to my mother last week.

b)
   i) If you don't answer this, I will start sending you the bills for the repairs to my car.
   ii) I will take further action if there is no response to this letter.
   iii) If there is no response to this letter, I intend to take the matter to 'The Investigators' on the ABC.

c)
   i) It is time something was done about your company.
   ii) It is time you seriously investigated the actions of your staff.
   iii) It is time someone took your company to court.

d)
   i) A while ago, I asked you to send me some things and you haven't.
   ii) On 17/7/87, I ordered three sets of Brito paints and I still haven't received them.
   iii) In July, I ordered some paint from you. I'm still waiting for it.

e)
   i) I can't believe an organization like yours could be so stupid.
   ii) I am amazed at your stupidity.
   iii) I am very surprised that a reputable organization like yours could take such action.

Exercise 4

Below is an incomplete draft of a letter of complaint. The writer has left blanks:
— where he was not sure about which word to use
— where he intended to add extra detail or comment
Revise the draft by adding whatever you think appropriate.

```
Dear Sir/Madam,

    I wish to complain about the noise from the night
football matches held at the Sydney Cricket Ground.
    I (i) ...................... that it is a popular sport and
that night football allows many more people to enjoy
matches. (ii) ......................, residents in the area also
need some (iii) ...................... of their rights.
    In the first place, it seems (iv) ...................... to
begin each match with firework displays and loud rock
music. Surely most people attend for the football, not
these extras.
    Secondly, the public address system seems (v) ...............
loud. I live at least 2 kilometres from the oval (vi) .......
..............................................................................
..............................................................................
    Finally, although I know it must be difficult to
control, (vii) ..............................................................
about the noisy and unruly crowds who wander the streets
afterwards?
    I myself enjoy a good football match so I am not
suggesting that the venue be closed to football. But I do
ask that the organizers (viii) ..............................................
..............................................................................
..............................................................................
                        Yours faithfully,
```

Exercise 5

Sometimes when you make a complaint on the telephone, you are told to 'put it in writing'. Look at this telephone conversation:

Consumer: Hello. I'd like to make a complaint about some of your paint I bought recently.

Switchboard: I'll put you through to the Manager's office.

Manager's office: Can I help you?

Consumer: Yes, look, I bought some of your 'all-weather exterior paint' recently and it's only lasted two months. It says on the tin it will last two years.

Manager's office: Where did you buy it?

Consumer: At Supaware, Marrickville. They told me they take no responsibility and that I should speak directly to you.

Manager's office: What's the problem?

Consumer:	Well, I painted my garage with it 2 months ago, and it's peeling already.
Manager's office:	We do take all such complaints very seriously, but the manager prefers to have them in writing. Can you write us a letter? Address it to the Manager and give all the details — where and when you bought it, when you used it and where — and so on. We'll discuss it fully when we get your letter. You see, it may be a problem with the surface, not the paint itself.
Consumer:	Well, I'm sure it's not, but I'll write to you immediately.

Write the letter required.
 — Begin by making notes of the parts of the conversation you will mention.
 — Draft the letter.
 — Revise as needed, and set out in the way shown in the Introduction.

Exercise 6

a) Look at the note below. It was written from one tenant to another in a large block of flats.

> 6th June
>
> Dear Neighbour,
>   I appreciate that you might want to leave your radio on while you are out — for security reasons — but would you mind not leaving it on quite so loudly in future. As I'm sure you're aware, sound travels very easily in this building and it's enough to cope with the noises people make when they're home!
>   Thanks for your cooperation.
>
> Van Nguyen
> (Flat 10)

b) Unfortunately, this note had no effect and the radio was left on more loudly. Write a second note to that tenant.
  — Use the information in the first note.
  — Mention that this is the second note.
  — Mention that you will write to the landlord or agent if this gets no response.

c) Your note gets no response, so you decide to write to the landlord or agent. Write the letter, including a mention of your two notes.

Exercise 7

Below are the notes a resident made when preparing to write a letter of protest about a proposed new freeway in his or her suburb.

Loss of homes
more traffic in surrounding streets
noise, pollution
no consultation with residents.
Why not put money into public transport?
only save motorists 2 minutes.
$200 million too much
Will take 8 years to build!

– Reorganize the notes into appropriate order.
– Draft the letter, adding your own comments.
– Revise as needed.

Exercise 8

Below are some words that are useful in letters of protest or complaint. Learn them using the ideas in Unit 4, *Spelling*.

bought	inconvenient	recently
purchase	realize	worth
warranty	appreciate	expensive
guarantee	afraid	enclosed
faulty	finally	trouble
poorly	refund	faithfully
designed	exchange	sincerely

Exercise 9

Below are some situations where letters of protest or complaint are appropriate. Choose one or two and write the letters.

a) You buy a toy truck as a Christmas present for a child. On Christmas Day, the child hurts him or herself badly when one finger is trapped between the wheels and body of the truck. You write to the manufacturer.

b) You come out of your house one morning to find a parking ticket for $25 on your car window. The ticket says your car was not close and parallel to the kerb. Your car is as close to the kerb as all the other cars in the street, and no other cars have tickets. Your car is parallel to the kerb, but the wheels are slightly turned outwards. You decide to protest about the fine.

c) Your child comes home from school with a note informing you that the school is closing at the end of the year because of falling numbers. All parents are asked to write and complain to the Department of Education, so you do so.

d) You have applied for a job. (Make up one relevant to your own situation.) You have suitable qualifications and experience. You do not get the job and are told it is because you are not the right sex / nationality / age / marital status (choose one). You decide to write a letter of protest to the Anti-Discrimination Board.

e) You find out that the Council plans to chop down all the trees in your street / build a supermarket next to your house / put 'No Parking' signs all along your street (choose one). You wish to protest and so decide to write a letter.

f) You share a small 2-bedroom flat with one other person. You receive a notice saying your rent will rise by $20 per week. You feel the rent rise is unfair for the following reasons:
   — the flat is in great need of repair
   — the last rent rise was 3 months ago
   — you are a very good tenant
   — the rise will mean you have to get a third tenant, and it is a very small flat.
   You write to the agent or to a residents' help organization. (Find out the name of one where you live.)

Exercise 10

Do you need or want to write a letter of protest or complaint? Write it now. Prepare by asking yourself some questions:
e.g. For a letter of complaint about something you bought:
   Where did I buy it?
   Who did I speak to?
and by making any other notes you feel necessary. Draft your letter and revise as needed.

13 Letters of opinion

Introduction

Have you ever felt strongly about a subject and wanted to write a letter to someone to express your opinion? Perhaps you have thought about writing a letter to:
- the editor of your class or school magazine
- the editor of a local newspaper
- your local Member of Parliament
- a political organization
- a government department
- the local council
- a community group.

Collect some examples of letters of opinion from the 'Letters to the Editor' sections of your local newspapers. They will be useful in some of the exercises in this unit.

Read the two 'Letters to the Editor' below, then discuss these questions:

i)   What is the common topic of the letters?
ii) Which letter was written in response to a previous letter? How can you tell?
iii) Why is letter B divided into paragraphs, while letter A is not?
iv) Which letter do you prefer and why?

LETTER A

Dear Editor,
  I was absolutely disgusted to hear that a young man, convicted of throwing a brick at a policeman and causing serious injury, was given a two year good behaviour bond. Where is the justice in our society? Why aren't violent criminals like this put in jail?
                 **Name and address
                        supplied**

LETTER B

Sir,

I was interested to read "Crime and Punishment" (Letters 26/5/88). Like Mr L. Smith, I am concerned about the light sentences given to many criminals.

I don't believe, however, that jail is always the best place, especially for young people. They may come out worse criminals than they were when they went in.

If we are serious about reducing crime, we should also do something about some of the causes, such as unemployment and poverty.

My suggestion is that we put criminals to work for the community in some way. Then we might all benefit.

A. Broom
Croydon

When writing letters of opinion:

i)   Follow the advice in Unit 10, *Formal letters*, to set out your letter. If your letter is published in a newspaper, it will usually be printed with just your name and suburb at the bottom (Letter B). You may request that none of this information is published (Letter A).

ii) Follow the advice in Unit 10, *Formal letters*, to begin your letter.

iii) If you are responding to another letter or article, say this in the opening sentence. Give details of the date, the title (if there is one) and the writer of that letter or article (Letter B).

iv) In a longer letter (Letter B):
   – make your topic and opinion clear in the first paragraph
   – organize your ideas into paragraphs to help the reader follow your arguments
   – restate your opinion, or offer a suggestion or warning in the last paragraph.

Exercise 1

The following letter appeared in the 'Letters to the Editor' section of a newspaper. Notice the organization of the letter into three paragraphs:
i)   an introduction (mentioning the topic and the writer's opinion)
ii) the reasons for the writer's opinion
iii) a conclusion (mentioning a final warning).

Sir,
   I know it is unfashionable to say so, but I believe that a woman's role is as wife and mother and that, wherever possible, she should stay home to look after her children.
   Many women nowadays say they have to go out to work so that the family can earn enough money. But I think they are too concerned about material possessions and not concerned enough about the welfare of their children. How can they be good mothers if they are not there when their children need them?
   If women continue to work, our children will continue to suffer, and so will our community.
                    (Mrs) J. Childs
                    Chatswood

Below is a draft of a letter written in response to the one above. Rewrite the letter.
– Add the necessary punctuation (see Unit 5, *Punctuation*).
– Organize the content into three paragraphs (an introduction, a middle and a conclusion).

Sir,

in reply to mrs childs' letter (12/4/88)
about working mothers i would like to say
that i totally disagree with her views
going out to work does not mean that your
children are left alone without caring
adults around them most working mothers are
very concerned that their children are well
looked after i would also like to add that
i am a working mother and that my children
are healthy happy well-behaved and much
loved if mrs childs thinks it is better
for her to stay home with her children
that's fine but she should allow other
women to make up their own minds

Exercise 2

Linking words and phrases help to make a piece of writing flow smoothly.

a) Look at this draft of a letter to a Parents and Friends Association. Take note of the linking words added.

19 Wallis Ave
Riverwood
Oct. 27th

Mrs B. Bartello
Secretary
Parents and Friends Association
Riverwood Primary School

Dear Mrs Bartello,

    I am writing in response to your last P&C newsletter in which you asked for parents' opinions on how to spend the $7,000 raised over the last 12 months.

    Firstly, I think that the library is in the most urgent need of more resources. And that at least $3,000 should be spent in this area, so that a large number of books, videos and cassettes can be bought.

    Secondly, Another personal computer for the children to use would be a worthwhile purchase, even though it would be quite expensive.

    Finally, There is a need for more playground equipment in the junior primary playground. And Repairs are also needed to some of the older equipment.

    Thank you for this opportunity to express my views. I know that whatever you decide, the school will benefit.

              Yours sincerely,

       (Mr) S. Savva

b) In this letter to the local council, some linking words and phrases are missing. Add appropriate words.

Dear Councillor,
    In a recent Council newsletter, we were concerned to read that the Council is considering a plan to pull down the old theatre in Broad Ave. In response to your request for residents' opinions, we are writing to express our strong objections to the plan.
    (i) .... we believe the theatre is a beautiful old building. It may need a few repairs, (ii) .... it is worth saving and restoring (iii) .... it adds a lot of charm to the area.
    (iv) ...., the theatre still serves a useful purpose. Many community groups hold their meetings there and it is (v) .... used for film nights, concerts, wedding receptions and parties.
    (vi) .... the theatre were to be destroyed, it would be very hard to find other suitable venues in the area. (vii) ...., we sincerely hope that you will vote against the plan in Council.
    Yours faithfully,

T O'Brien

T. O'Brien
Secretary,
Randwick Residents Group

Exercise 3

In the following letter to his local Member of Parliament, the writer expresses his opinion on keeping dolphins and seals in captivity. Rearrange the parts into the correct order.

RELEASE THE DOLPHINS

Dear Mrs Chapman,

i) I was especially upset to see dolphins and seals kept in small ponds. They looked bored and lifeless and it is no wonder.

ii) If it is possible to do so, we should return these animals to the wild.

iii) I am writing to express my opinion on keeping dolphins and seals in captivity.

iv) These animals would normally be in family groups roaming great distances across the seas, not isolated in pools 12 metres wide by 5 metres deep.

v) If not, we should at least ensure that no more dolphins and seals are captured for animal parks.

vi) I recently visited the Pitman Wildlife Park and I was disgusted with the conditions I saw there.

Yours sincerely,

Exercise 4

Imagine your school or educational institution is considering a plan to:
— stop students smoking in the students' common room
— make students do work in the community for two hours per week
— take away the students' common room to make a much needed extra
   classroom, or
— fine students for being late to class.
You have been asked to write to your school magazine, giving your opinion.

a) Choose one of the above and follow the ideas in Units 1, 2 and 3, *Preparing to write, Drafting* and *Revising*, to write your letter.
   Use the following outline if you like:

Dear Mr/Mrs/Ms ....
In response to your request for opinions on the plan to ....
....
......................., I would like to say that I strongly agree/disagree.
   In the first place, ...
....
....
   Secondly, ...
....
....
   In conclusion then, ...
....
Yours sincerely,

b) Check your letter for spelling errors.
   — Underline any words you think *look* wrong, or any words you were unable to spell.
   — Follow the ideas in Unit 4, *Spelling*, to correct them.
   — Check your spelling using a dictionary.

Exercise 5

These pictures are from the cover of a motorists' magazine. They show Australian families on holiday. Why do you think they made some readers angry?

Read the following letter written in response to the pictures. Then write your own letter to the editor expressing *your* opinion.

Women's holiday role

I must protest at the cover of the December issue. The pictures suggest that for a good 'Aussie' holiday, not only is a caravan necessary, but also a piece of feminine baggage, who will be useful to do the washing, mind the kids, wash the dishes, etc., while dad and the kids relax and have a holiday.

I would like to suggest that many husbands would be offended. They take pride in giving their wives a holiday and do most of the household tasks during the holiday.

This picture of Australian family life is outdated and offensive. An apology to your readers is called for.

Mr N. Lowie
Mt Pleasant

Exercise 6

Read the articles below and choose one that interests you. Write a letter to the editor of your class magazine or the editor of these newspapers, expressing your opinion on the subject.

Follow the ideas in Units 1, 2 and 3, *Preparing to write*, *Drafting* and *Revising* to write your letter. (In your opening sentence mention the article you are responding to.)

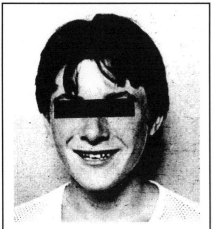

The 15-year-old who divorced his parents

IN Melbourne, a 15-year-old schoolboy was granted a divorce – from his parents.

The Children's Court was told he had irreconcilable differences with his parents because they punished him for wagging school.

Victorian parents were jumping up and down on Thursday, following the schoolboy's divorce, and claiming the State's Children's court was splitting up families.

What would we do without TV?

Research from America shows that children as young as two are watching 30 hours of television a week. These findings have shocked many communities across the country into taking action. In Farmingdale, New Jersey, for example, thousands of families have agreed not to turn on their television sets for one month and to record the effect this has on their lives. Already there are reports of increased anxiety, sleeplessness, child misbehaviour and violence; a 10-year-old boy was caught breaking down the door of a locked room to get at the TV.

Daily Observer, 14.11.87

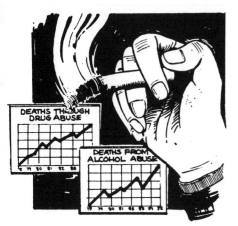

A report published in the July issue of the Journal of Medicine finds that cigarette companies are fighting back against the anti-smoking lobbies. Cigarette companies have been sponsoring sporting events, art exhibitions and medical research to improve their public image.

Herald, 19.8.86

Exercise 7

Collect some interesting 'Letters to the Editor' from your local newspapers. Write a reply to a letter of your choice. You may agree or disagree with the original writer.

Here are some examples to begin with.

Good news?

Isn't it about time we had some good news in the paper? It seems to be the policy of all newspapers to only publicize crime and bad news. Surely there must be some good news that deserves publicity. It would make a nice change.

N. Hakim
Nth Hobart

Cars too fast

Sir, I agree with M. Mallot (6/2/88) regarding slowing cars down. It has been proven that speeds kill. So why do we keep making cars that go faster? If the speed limit is 110km/hr, why do we need cars that go 200km/hr?

Mr W. Enderby
Moonee Ponds

LANDLORDS say that they do not get enough back from their investments and that they must increase rents sharply in order to survive.

In 35 years I have never met a landlord who was going broke and I believe that the current rent increases are unfair.

My rent has just gone up by $15/week and this is the second rise in 18 months. The place needs repairs and nothing has been done for years. Come on landlords, give us a fair deal!

H. Owens
Glenelg

Exercise 8

Think of an issue that concerns you at the moment and that you would like to write about. It could be a local, national or international issue.

Write a letter expressing your opinion. (Decide first who you should write to.)

Here are a few ideas to begin with.

— The behaviour of school children on public transport
— Childcare facilities: their cost and availability
— The use of drugs by sportsmen and women to improve their performances
— The standard of children's television programs
— The use of the death penalty for serious crimes
— Government support for the unemployed
— The development of nuclear weapons
— The vandalizing of telephone boxes
— The commercialization of Christmas
— The pollution of the environment
— Payment for housework
— The reintroduction of fees for tertiary study.

CREATIVE WRITING CONTEXTS

14 Personal writing

Introduction

Personal writing is writing you do for yourself rather than for someone else to read. It could be:
- a diary to keep a record of daily events
- a travel diary to keep a record of a holiday or trip
- a study diary to keep a record of what you have been learning
- a problem diary to write about your problems in order to understand them better, or
- a reminder note to help you remember something.

Because you are writing for yourself, you can write whatever you like, in whatever way you like.

Look at the two examples of diary writing below. Notice the different styles used by the two writers.

Weather is cold + wet — winter has arrived! Good news — Rosa + Eduardo have just had a baby girl — Mother + daughter both well. Have not decided on a name yet. Will visit her next week. Took the dogs for a run in the park. Couldn't stay long —too cold!

I went to visit my father-in-law today. Its lovely to sit and talk to him. He has so many stories to tell. I've tried to persuade him to write down his memoirs but he says he's just lived an ordinary life.
Today he was telling me about the time that he and his younger brother ran away from home. He was only 9 years old at the time. They decided they were going to have an adventure so they took a bundle of food and clothes and...

Exercise 1

Sometimes the hardest part of diary writing is deciding what to write about. Try one of these ideas today and the others in the days to come.

a) Think of three people that you came into contact with today. They may be people you know well, or they may be strangers. They may be people that you spoke to or just people that you noticed on the bus. Do two minutes speed writing on each person. Write about:
   – what they looked like
   – what they were doing
   – why you remember them.
   For notes on speed writing, see Unit 1, *Preparing to write*.

b) Think over your day.
   – What was the most enjoyable hour in your day? Why? What happened?
   – Write about it for at least three minutes
   – What was the worst hour in your day? Why? What happened?
   – Write about it for at least three minutes.

c) Choose a few of the following words (or add others of your choice) that best describe your day.

exciting	frustrating	romantic
ordinary	disastrous	exhausting
tiring	emotional	interesting
busy	dull	boring
fun	stressful	normal
terrifying	wonderful	sociable
relaxing	extraordinary	pleasant

   Beside each word you choose, write a short note to explain your choice. e.g.

   > Busy – I had to finish writing the report by 5 o'clock. I got it done – but I didn't even have time for lunch.
   >
   > Relaxing – slept in this morning – too cold to get out of bed. Spent most of the day reading and listening to music.

d) Think over your day. Make a list of things that happened in the order that they happened. Write about these things now, adding details and comments.

e) Use one of these openings to begin your diary entry.
   'I heard on the news today that . . .'
   'I saw . . . today. She/he said . . .'

Exercise 2

Begin to keep a regular diary of daily events. Use some of the ideas you have practised in exercise 1 to help you write.

Exercise 3

Look at this page from a travel diary.

Nov. 12th

Today I travelled across the island to a small village called San Cristobel. It's not much more than 20 buildings along a dusty street – full of children and dogs. I'm staying in the "Hotel Cristobel" – the only one in town. The word "hotel" makes it sound somewhat grander than it is. It's a dilapidated 2 storey building – with old wooden shutters hanging from the windows. But the rooms are cool and from my window I can see the sea and the fishing boats coming and going.

a) If you have some photographs or souvenirs from a recent holiday, use them to help you recall events. Write about some things that happened.

b) Keep a travel diary when you next go on holiday.

Exercise 4

Look at the example of a study diary below.

Today we read a story from an Italian magazine and then discussed it (in Italian of course). At first everyone was very self-conscious and nobody wanted to talk – but gradually the discussion got going – and then the teacher couldn't stop us. It was fun. I hope we do it again next week.
At times I still translate in my head – but I'm getting better at thinking in Italian.

If you are attending classes at the moment, or teaching yourself to do something, keep a record of what you are learning and how you feel about it. These questions may help you.
– What did I learn today?
– How much time did I spend on it?
– Did I enjoy it? Why/why not?
– What was difficult? What was easy?
– Any other comments?

Exercise 5

Look at the example of a problem diary below.

When she told me I went cold all over —
kind of numb — I didn't want to believe
it and I just kept saying No-No! Then
it was as though my whole world had
collapsed — an awful feeling like I was
— I don't know — being buried or something.
It was later that I started to feel angry
— really angry — thinking why should this happen
to me.

When you have a personal problem, writing about it can often help you cope.
It may help you to understand your feelings better and to find a solution to the
problem.

Exercise 6

Look at these examples of reminder notes.

a) THURSDAY

    — pick up photos ✓
    — send cheque to Telecom
    — take suit to Dry Cleaners ✓
    — Ring Mum
    — Hairdressers — <u>2.30</u>

b) Don't forget
  — hat
  — sunburn cream
  — moisturizer
  — mosquito repellent
  — anti-bacterial powder
  — mosquito net
  — cassette player/cassettes/batteries
  — camera
  — diary

Think of some things you must remember to do over the next few days. Write
yourself reminder notes.

15 Stories

Introduction

The stories you write may be about events from your own life, or from your imagination. You may choose to write them for yourself, for friends and family to read, or for wider publication, for example in a school magazine. (If possible, organize such a school magazine.)

Here is a useful plan to follow to make your stories interesting to read. Include:

i) An *orientation* or introduction.
    Here the writer explains who the story is about (the main character or characters), and perhaps where the story takes place (the setting).
ii) A *complication* or middle part.
    Here the main events of the story unfold and some problem or crisis occurs.
iii) A *resolution* or conclusion.
    Here the problem or crisis is resolved.

Notice the orientation, the complication and the resolution in this very short story found in a newspaper.

Panic in love nest

Orientation	The man of the house had left for work, and there she was, trapped in the second floor flat without a key.
Complication	The real trouble was, she was his mistress, and his wife was due home at any minute. Frantic, she dialled 000 and explained her predicament to the fire brigade.
Resolution	Firemen sped to the scene and brought her down by ladder, and off she went, just in time.

Now read the short story below. In groups, discuss which is the orientation, the complication and the resolution of the story.

Hero or fool?

I went to the bank as usual last Thursday to cash my pay cheque. There were perhaps twenty people waiting in line for the tellers, and I joined the queue.

Suddenly three men burst through the door. They were wearing balaclavas over their heads and carrying guns. They yelled at everyone to move back against the wall. One of them stood by the door. Another jumped over the counter and forced the tellers to put cash into a carry bag. A third stood facing us, gun in hand. He looked quite young and extremely nervous.

Within just a few minutes they were ready to leave. Two ran out the door, carrying the bag, and jumped into a waiting car. The third, the young one, hesitated for a moment, then he too turned to run out the door.

I don't know what came over me. Suddenly I jumped at him and pushed him to the floor. He dropped the gun and another customer picked it up and threw it across the room. The car outside sped off as the two of us sat on our captive until the police arrived to make an arrest.

Exercise 1

Read the short story below several times. Try to remember as much of the story as you can.

Alfonso

The famous movie star, Alfonso, had lived in seclusion for many years because he was afraid of being mobbed by his adoring fans. He never went out, not even to the shops. He had everything he needed delivered to the house.

After five years of this, however, he began to miss the contact with other people. He wanted to be the centre of attention once more. So he decided to visit a restaurant where he had once been a well-known customer.

It was a disastrous decision. Not one person recognized him. He returned home even lonelier than before.

Cover the story and rewrite it from memory. Keep as close to the original as possible.

Compare your story with the original. Does your story have (i) an orientation, (ii) a complication, (iii) a resolution?

Exercise 2

Think of a story that you know well. It may be one that you remember from childhood, a book you have read or a movie you have seen recently.
– Rehearse the story in your head.
– Tell the outline of the story to another student. Leave out all the details.
– Write down the outline of the story in about 50 words.
– Keep your outline to use in exercise 6.

Exercise 3

Read the opening paragraph (the orientation) of a short story, below.

Helena Davros lived with her husband and two children in a small flat above a take-away food shop in a suburb of Melbourne. She was a quiet woman. Nothing much seemed to worry her and she went about her life without worrying other people. She lived a very ordinary life until one day last June, when all that changed.

– Discuss what you think might happen in the rest of the story.
– Write an outline of the rest of the story in about 50 words. Keep this outline to use in exercise 6.

Exercise 4

In the following short story the ending (the resolution) is missing. Discuss with other students possible ways to finish the story. Then write an ending.

Kata

When I was growing up, I lived with my mother, my sister and my brother in a small village. We were very poor. My father had died during the war and my mother found it very hard to support us. She always made sure we had food to eat, but she could not save enough money to pay the rates on our small farm.

I remember one cold grey day a man came to the farm and argued with my mother about money. She tried to explain that we had none. He went away again, but several days later three men arrived. They walked straight up to the barn, led the cow out and loaded it onto a truck. Then they took the pigs. Finally they went inside the house and took away my mother's sewing machine.

Our lives changed greatly that day. Our mother cried bitterly as she packed a small bag with our clothes. She took us to our grandmother's house. She kissed us all and left us there.

We waited for days for her to return and take us back to our farm, but she didn't come. Nobody talked about it. We were all too worried and sad. Then about two months later . . .

Exercise 5

Think of a topic on which to write a true story. It can be a story about your own life or about someone you know. Follow these steps to write your story.

i)   Preparing to write
     – Rehearse the outline of the story. You may do this in your head, talking to other students, talking into a cassette or writing on paper.
     – Keep your story simple at this stage.

ii) Drafting
     – Write a first draft of your story. See the suggestions in Unit 2, *Drafting*.
     – Write quickly. Don't worry about neatness and correctness.
     – When you have finished a first draft, put it aside for a few days before you begin to revise it.

iii) Revising
     – Use the suggestions in Unit 3, *Revising*, to help you improve your story.
     – Check that your story has an orientation, a complication and a resolution.
     – Make any changes you think will improve your story.
     – Finally, write out your story neatly.

Exercise 6

Reread the story outlines you wrote in exercises 2 and 3. Choose one and write the full story. Draft and revise as in exercise 5 above.

Exercise 7

Newspaper articles sometimes suggest interesting stories. Use the events in the cartoon and article below as the basis for a story. You might write it from the viewpoint of the zoo keeper, a visitor to the zoo, or even the orangutan!

Bars? Humbug!

Ken-Allan, a 14-year-old orangutan from Borneo, has been confined to his quarters at the San Diego Zoo.

His crime: attempted escape.

Ken-Allan found a workman's crowbar, hid it and – with a female accomplice named Vicki – used it to crack a plexiglass window.

Zoo authorities said it was his third escape bid this year.

Find other interesting articles in your local newspapers to use as the basis for story writing.

Exercise 8

Choose one or more of the following ideas for story writing.

a) Write a story that includes one of these sentences:
    'Slowly and very carefully he picked it up and gave it to her.'
    'She ran for the door but found it was locked.'
    'I couldn't find them anywhere.'

b) Write a story to illustrate a proverb, for example:
   'A stitch in time saves nine.'
   'Too many cooks spoil the broth.'
   'Look before you leap.'

c) These advertisements appeared in a newspaper. Choose one and write the story behind the advertisement.

LOST: One pair of men's trousers, somewhere in the city, around midnight last Saturday. Phone 330 3386.

d) Write a story to accompany the picture below.

e) Write a story beginning with one of the following:
   'It all happened so quickly . . . '
   'When I first arrived in this country . . . '.
   'I've met some interesting people in my time but X was something special . . . '

16 *Extras*

Introduction

This unit contains suggestions for 'fun' writing. In some of the exercises you will need to work in pairs or small groups.

Exercise 1

Written conversations
Work in pairs. Do *not* talk to your partner, but have a conversation in writing.
— Use one piece of paper.
— Student A writes a message and passes it to Student B.
— Student B reads the message, writes a reply and passes it back to Student A, and so on.
— Keep going for as long as you like, but for at least 5 minutes.
Remember *no talking*!

Exercise 2

Expanding sentences
Work in pairs or small groups. Find an interesting headline from the newspaper.
e.g. 'Woman finds $10,000'
     'Crocodile bites man'
     'Boy rescued from river'

— Rewrite the headline as a complete sentence. You may need to change some words.
  e.g. 'A woman found $10,000.'
— Take it it turns to add one piece of information to the same sentence. You may add to the beginning, the middle or the end.
  e.g. 'Yesterday a woman found $10,000.'
       'Yesterday a 64-year-old woman found $10,000.'
       'Yesterday a 64-year-old woman found $10,000 in a biscuit tin.'
— Continue until your sentence is as long as possible.

Exercise 3

Disappearing sentences
For this exercise you will need a long sentence containing a lot of information.
(You could use, for example, the expanded sentence made by another group of
students for exercise 2 above, or the opening sentence from a newspaper article.)
Work in pairs or small groups.
— In turn, take out one piece of information from the sentence.
    e.g. 'A young man had a narrow escape from death today when he fell from
          a moving train at Healesville, north of Melbourne.'
        'A man had a narrow escape from death today when he . . . ' ('young'
          omitted)
        'A man had a narrow escape from death when he . . . ' ('today' omitted)
— Continue until the sentence is as short as possible.

Exercise 4

Linking ideas
Work in groups of four to six. Choose one of the following topics for your
group to write about.
'Parents' 'Drugs' 'Computers' 'Sport' 'Music' 'Spiders'
— Each person writes a simple one-idea-sentence on that topic.
— Collect all the sentences on the board or on a piece of paper.
— Write one or two paragraphs to include all the ideas collected. You will need
  to add linking words, rearrange the order and leave out some words to make
  your paragraphs flow smoothly.
— Compare your paragraphs with those of other groups.
e.g.

SOLAR ENERGY

1. *My neighbour has a solar energy hot water system in her
    house.*
2. *Solar energy is an alternative source of energy to gas,
    electricity and oil.*
3. *Solar energy is cheap.*
4. *Someone has designed a car that uses solar energy.*
5. *Solar energy can be used for many different purposes.*
6. *I don't know much about solar energy.*

*I don't know much about solar energy except that it is a cheap
alternative to gas, electricity and oil, and that it can be used
for many different purposes. My neighbour, for example, has a
solar energy hot water system and I believe that someone has
designed a solar-powered car.*

Exercise 5

Writing newspaper stories
— Cut out an interesting headline and story from an old newspaper.
— Paste the headline only on a sheet of paper. Underneath, write the question
  words 'Who?', 'Where?', 'When?', 'What?'.

e.g.

Lost boys found

who?

where?

when?

what?

— Exchange your headline and questions with another student. (Keep the story
  to read later.)
— Under the headline you receive, make up short answers to the questions.
— Then combine your answers to make one complete sentence. This will be the
  opening sentence of your news story.

e.g.

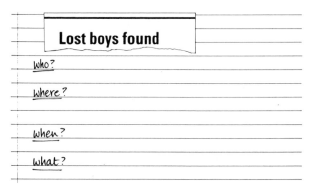

Lost boys found

Who?   2 boys, aged 10 and 12

Where?   in the bush, in the Dandenong Ranges,
         near Melbourne

When?   lost yesterday. Found this morning

what?   wandered away from a family picnic

Two boys, aged 10 and 12, who wandered away
from a family picnic in the Dandenong Ranges
near Melbourne yesterday, were found this
morning after spending all night in the bush.

— In the rest of your story explain some of the events in more detail.
— Now compare your story with the original.

Exercise 6

Writing descriptions
Look at the advice given by 'Neighbourhood Watch' to help you keep your
neighbourhood more secure.

Neighbourhood watch
N.S.W. POLICE
WORKING TOGETHER
COMMUNITY CARING
COMMERCIAL UNION INSURANCE
NRMA INSURANCE

Remember, a patrolling police officer may not recognize a stranger in your neighbourhood, but you and your neighbours will.

Become the eyes and ears of the police, join the Neighbourhood Watch Program.

WRITE IT DOWN
Suspicious Persons
Sex; Age; Height; Build; Complexion; Hair colour/ style; Peculiarities (e.g. beard, moustache, tattoos, etc.)

a) Follow the points given and write descriptions of people (other students in the class, family, etc.).
  e.g. He is 22 to 23, 180cm (6ft) tall, with a solid build, olive complexion and dark brown curly hair. He is wearing blue jeans, a dark blue jumper and has gold chains around his neck.

b) Write a description of someone in your class. Read your description for others to guess who it is.

Exercise 7

Writing for advice
Many newspapers have advice columns where you can write for advice on a range of subjects including: education, health, gardening, pets and personal relationships.
e.g.

I am a 21-year-old woman from a European background. I still live with my parents but next year I plan to travel overseas with two girlfriends. I am really looking forward to it. Unfortunately, my parents are very much against it. They think I should stay home and wait for marriage. We have had some terrible arguments about it. How can I make them see that I need some independence? Am I being unreasonable? What should I do?   **Troubled**

● EDUCATION
WITH **BARRY DWYER,** EDUCATION AUTHOR

Q I WOULD like to buy a home computer as an aid to my child's education. Is there any general advice you can give me?

A For a start, don't rush off to the nearest store and make a hasty purchase.

You might begin by talking with friends who have already bought a computer; they will be able to tell you some of the pitfalls and give some indication of how their children use it.

More and more teachers are doing short courses in computer education. So you're quite likely to find someone on the staff of your child's school who would be able to offer specific advice with both the child and the computer in mind. Try to clarify in your own mind just what you hope to get from your new computer. A lot of parents are eventually disappointed because they expect too much from this new technology.

Do you need advice on any subject? Write a letter to the advice column in a local newspaper or magazine.

Exercise 8

Other ideas from the newspaper
Choose one of the ideas below for a 'fun' writing exercise.

What do you hate most about our wonderful city?

Sydney may be a wonderful place to live — the best address in the world. But every city has its problems and we all have things we hate about our city.

It could be the destruction of our old buildings, our sometimes uncaring attitude to the homeless, the pollution of our beaches or a host of other problems.

What do *you* hate most about Sydney? Agenda needs its readers to have a gripe — explaining what they dislike most about Sydney and what they would do about it.

Send your note to Agenda's Platform, GPO Box 506 Sydney 2001. Please include a phone number in case we need to check any details.

Write about the city *you* live in.

It's service with a snarl

WHATEVER happened to service? We all know the horror stories: the service stations that refuse to serve; the tradespeople who keep you waiting all day and then don't turn up; the long search for help in department stores which look like they've been hit by a lightning strike.

Sometimes the world seems full of surly waiters, gossiping shop assistants and companies that don't seem very interested in accepting your trade.

Then there are the scores of companies that refuse to fix a time for their house call — no doubt still dreaming of a world in which every **home has a woman waiting for a call.**

Write down your own experiences and send them to: Agenda's Platform, GPO Box 506, Sydney 2001. Include your phone number in case we want to check any details, and please post your note before the end of the week.

Meanwhile, we'll start collecting the excuses from the people who haven't been serving us.

Cat Lovers If you are over 20 years, male or female, own a cat and feed it an amount of canned cat food, we would like to talk to you about the possibility of doing some TV work. No experience required. Please write, including phone number, a recent photo of yourself (and if possible a photo of your cat or cats as well) and stating how much and which canned foods you feed it (them). We are especially interested to hear of any humorous or unusual thing your cat may do to attract your attention, amuse you or tell you its feeding time. If your cat's entertaining or simply lovable – don't delay, we'd like to hear from you now.

Write to: Cat Lovers
P.O. Box 941, North Sydney 2060   P670

Do you live like Krystle?

How different is your life from *Dynasty's* beautiful and wealthy Krystle Carrington, played by Linda Evans.

Let us know and you'll be in the running to win a fabulous new perfume called *Forever Krystle*, valued at $120 for 25 ml.

We all know Krystle looks like a million dollars in silk from dawn till dusk, that she's sophisticated, warm, feminine and a breath of fresh air in an often cut-throat, ruthless family. Does that sound like you?

All you have to do to enter our contest is to tell us in no more than 50

CONTEST

words how your life is different from Krystle's.

Send your entries, including your name and address, to Scent Contest, *The Sun-Herald,* Box 7025, GPO Sydney, 2001. No correspondence will be entered into.

All entries must be received by Wednesday, September 4, and we will announce the winner on Sunday, September 8.

LINDA Evans as Krystle Carrington.

Are you a television addict dying to have your say? Do you have a literary bent, combined with a talent for criticising what you see? If so, this page belongs to you.

The *Canberra Chronicle* wants your point of view on television in Canberra. Put your comments on paper and send them to the *Canberra Chronicle,* PO Box 218, Canberra City. Readers whose views are published will win Systems 9 Lotto tickets, with the chance to win so much money that you will probably be able to afford to buy a television network yourself!

Write about television in *your* city or town. Here is what one person wrote.

I spend a good deal of time alone in the house, so television is important to me.

News is best on SBS. Here, without waste of time, we get straight facts. Not a detailed interpretation by someone else. Not a string of opinions. Not loud, urgent, noisy. We can see a map of where overseas events are taking place – very much appreciated if your geography is a bit rusty. Certainly more agreeable than the guns, coffins, funerals and fights which leave me with the impression that the whole world is a battlefield.

YOUR NEWS

TELL us what is happening in your suburb by writing to this newspaper, PO Box 21, Waterloo 2017, or telephone 662-8888.

WANTED

Do you have that certain yearning to have your written words published?

The Surry Cosmopolitan **welcomes all submissions from the local community irrespective of content or topic.**

No guarantee is given that what you send will be printed but why not give it a try – remember this is a community newspaper – your newspaper.

Answers

1   Preparing to write

Exercise 7

Phrases used to introduce and link the writer's three arguments:
   In the first place
   What's more
   And then

3. Revising

Exercise 1

a) Here is one possible answer:

The Club will hold a fireworks display on Saturday, 28th November at 8pm. It will celebrate our 10th anniversary! The display will be held at the north end of the O'Connell Oval. All members and their friends are welcome to attend. There will be a small charge of $2 per adult (children free) to cover food and drink.

If you are coming, please tell the Secretary by 20th November.

b) Here is one possible answer:

Last Monday the Socceroos played in Birmingham against Aston Villa. They played well, <u>but</u> luck was not on their side <u>and</u> they were defeated. <u>However</u>, that was their first defeat in this world tour. They must play five or six more games in the UK and Europe <u>before</u> they return home on September 19th. Their next match is against Manchester United. <u>Although</u> this is expected to be a close match, the Socceroos are tipped to win.

c) Here is one possible answer:

26 January

Dear Eddie,
Here in Perth, it's sunny and warm. I arrived yesterday at 3pm and already have a suntan. It's a nice change from the cold, grey days at home. The hotel is very close to the beach. I was lucky enough to get a room with a view. I expect to be here till the end of the month. Then I'll get the train across to Sydney. See you then.
Lee.

d) Here is one possible answer:

Suddenly the phone rang. The mother rushed to answer it. The family waited in silence. They could barely hear her when she finally spoke. 'Willy, it's for you.' He hesitated for a second and then grabbed the phone from her. He listened for a long while. His face was expressionless. At last he spoke, but they were unable to catch what he said. Suddenly he slammed down the receiver, got his coat and left silently.

e) Here are some possible answers:

i) *Has Jana rung you from Newcastle? I have a feeling she has not got your number so here is hers — 049 621723. She and Simon will be in Melbourne on approximately 17th Dec. What a shame you're not here too. They would love to see you, I know.*

ii) *I am checking my report now and think it will be finished by Christmas. I can't quite believe it!!*

iii) *Thanks for the video. We haven't actually got a video machine yet but perhaps we'll have to get one now.*

iv) *Perhaps we'll come for a holiday to Darwin sometime if you are still there.*

f) Here is one way to combine each pair:
i) *Personal letter*
I'm glad to hear that you are well and that everything is going well with the business.
ii) *Job application*
I have enjoyed working here for the past three years, but now I'm looking for a change from hotel work.

iii) *Letter of protest*
I was particularly upset because my young children were watching TV at the time.

iv) *Personal letter*
Like me, he is from the south, so we have something in common.

v) *Formal letter*
Please find enclosed a cheque for $18 which is the deposit for the workshop on August 23rd.

g) Here is one way to divide each sentence:

i) *News report for a school magazine*
A severe thunderstorm passed through Sydney around noon yesterday, flooding some city streets and disrupting traffic. It caused widespread damage especially in the Hurstville area where many trees were uprooted, roofs blown off and power lines brought down.

ii) *Letter of opinion*
Given the extent of the shoplifting problem these days, I think it is quite reasonable for store management to carry out bag searching. However, I do think it is essential that there are warning signs and that the searches are done in a polite way. If this is done, customers have no cause for complaint.

4 Spelling

Exercise 3

a) height   fluency
    patient   pursuit
    emergency   desperate
    detergent   breathe

b) listen   foreign
    chaos   vehicle
    calm   doubt
    whether   receipt

c) applied   budgeted   changed
    applying   budgeting   changing
    occurred   paid   tied
    occurring   paying   tying
    shopped   believed   danced
    shopping   believing   dancing

Exercise 6

b) incidences   painfully
    highest   sunburned
    skinned   infection
    periods   serious
    generally   attention

5 Punctuation

Exercise 1

I wish to apply for the clerical position advertised in "The Canberra Times", Saturday, 31st January. At present I am working for the Department of Finance.

Although I have only been there since November, I have gained a wide variety of experience in clerical duties. In addition, I worked for the ABC for one year as a pay clerk in 1984.

Exercise 2

What would you do if you saw a snake?
The safest thing to do is avoid it. Snakes are naturally shy of humans who are a threat to them. Their first form of defence is to move away from danger. They will not deliberately chase humans but if provoked or cornered they may attempt to bite. Snakes are protected in all states and territories of Australia and may not be killed unless they threaten life.

Exercise 3

What is W.I.R.E.?
Who needs W.I.R.E.?
How can I stop my boss from annoying me?
Why am I finding it hard to get social security?
Where do I go for legal help?
What do I do if my ex-husband won't leave me alone?
Who can help me if my landlord threatens to evict me and my children?
Do I have to speak English to be understood on the telephone?

Exercise 4

Exclamation marks could go after:
. . . injury!
. . . booming!
. . . goodness!
. . . to pay!
. . . loved it!

Exercise 5

Message from the Editor

This is the last issue of the Post before Christmas, so I would like to take the opportunity of wishing readers a happy Christmas.
   I would also like to take the opportunity to thank all those people who have helped the Post this year. These people give their time voluntarily to organise distribution, letterbox, write articles, chase up information and advertisements, take photographs and prepare the paper for the printer. I think you will agree they do a great job.
   That's all for this year. See you in 1989.

The Editor

Exercise 6

a) my boyfriend's father
b) Peter's brother
c) my friends' house
d) the students' association
e) the foreman's office
f) the men's changing room
g) Ross's office
h) the sportswomen's club

Exercise 7

mightn't, I'll, I've, can't, you'll, that'll, all's

Exercise 8

I couldn't let her go without a word. "Will you return?" I asked. "Never," was the short reply. She saw the distress on my face. "Look," she said, "I don't mean to hurt you. I just can't see any other way. It seems hopeless." I knew she was right.

Exercise 9

. . . (it sounds urgent).
. . . (−6° this morning) . . .

Exercise 10

Are you planning to go into the bush this summer? Remember to take a safety kit which contains:
– a map and compass
– waterproof matches in a waterproof container
– solid fuel firelighter or candle
– a whistle
– a mirror for emergency signalling
– a small notebook and pencil
– a knife or other sharp instrument
– a cup or container
– water sterilization tablets
– a first aid kit
– a torch.

Exercise 11

The Times

OCTOBER/NOVEMBER

Editorial

On the last Sunday of October the clocks are changed in most of Australia.

In all states except for Queensland and Western Australia clocks and watches are put forward by one hour. For example, 9 in the morning becomes 10. We call this daylight saving, because we make better use of the increased daylight hours in the longer summer days. People can enjoy sporting and outdoor activities until quite late each evening.

Enjoy the extra daylight while it lasts because, on the first Sunday of March, everyone will have to put the hands of their watches and clocks back again, and get up in the dark.

See you next edition!

Lygon Street Festa

The Lygon Street Festa takes place on Saturday the 11th and Sunday the 12th of November in Carlton. There are many Italian shops and cafes in Lygon Street so the Festa has an Italian flavour. However, many other ethnic groups take part in the two days of celebrations. There is music, dancing, and all kinds of food as well as fun and games for the kids. You can get free programs on the day.

But one warning. If you want a quiet weekend then stay at home! You'll find almost as many people in this one street as at the Melbourne Cup!

Melbourne Cup

Australia's greatest horse racing event is held on the first Tuesday in November at Flemington Race Course and the distance is 3200m (2 miles). Melbourne is the only place in the world that has a public holiday for a horse race!

The first Cup was run in 1861. That year there were 17 horses in the race and 4,000 people attended. These days there are about 25 horses running and often more than 100,000 people at the Melbourne Cup. Many more thousands of people stay home and watch it on television or listen to it on the radio.

6 Postcards

Exercise 1

a) Here are some possibilities:
   i) Beautiful isn't it – it really looks like the picture too – green hills and blue sky as far as the eye can see. We are staying in an old farmhouse which has been turned into a small hotel – very comfortable. I'm in no hurry to leave.
   ii) I hope you are still having a good time in Italy. Angela gave me her sister's address to send to you. She said to visit her when you are in Ancona – it's 48 Via Fontana – her name is Luisa Vincenza. Stay in touch.

b) i) 6/697 Military Rd
       Mosman
       NSW 2088
       Australia

   ii) 22 North St
       Heidelburg
       Victoria 3084

   iii) 5/17 Mitchell Rd
        Sandy Bay
        Tasmania 5007

   iv) 81 Wesley Drive
       Titirangi
       New Zealand

Exercise 3

b) There are many possibilities. Here is one example:
   Having a great time – wish you could be here. Staying in a small boarding house near the lake – a very friendly place. Plan to stay here till early in August and then I'll fly to Adelaide. Still able to put me up for a while? Hope so. Will contact you again before I leave.

Exercise 4

Here is one possible way to shorten the letter:

Dear . . .
Unfortunately our holiday is almost over – a wonderful 3 weeks – weather has been great. Every day at the beach, bush-walking, driving in the hills, or long walks along the coast – wonderful scenery! Lots of photos to show you. In the evenings, magnificent sunsets and so many stars! Sadly we leave on Saturday. Will ring when we get back.
Love, Miriam

7 Notes and messages

Exercise 3

Here is one possible answer:

Wed. 10 am.

Alan,

Patricia rang to ask me to leave you this note – she tried to call you but there was no answer. She said to tell you that her plane won't get in till 10pm not 9pm as she thought. She still wants you to meet her – if you can't can you leave a message at the airport.

Josie.

Exercise 5

Here are possible answers:

Jenny rang – about 11. Ring her before leaving – URGENT.

Tools behind garage door. Careful of BIG spider in L-hand corner – might be dangerous. What do you think?

Out of everything!! If hungry – stale bread in tin and Vegemite in top cupboard. If you can't last till 10, get take-away from corner shop – must fly now.

John called – party tonight – 1/130 Blair St, Newtown. I'll be there about 9. Should be good! Can you bring wine??

Camping trip off! Call you later – too hard to explain now.

Sorry about mess. Been searching for 1½ hours for socks – can't even find a DIRTY pair – what have you done with them all?? I'll clean up later.

Exercise 6

a) ii) Bill and Lina are probably living or staying in the same place and know each other well (e.g. husband/wife, boyfriend/girlfriend, brother/sister, close friends or house/flatmates).

Chris and Lina are also probably living or staying in the same place, but either do not know each other well (e.g. house/flatmates but not close friends, house guest/house resident) or are of different ages (older relative/younger relative) or both.

b) ii) Liz and Rob and Marisa may be living in the same place, or in close proximity (same block of flats, same street) but either do not know each other well or are of different ages, or both.

      Janie and Rob and Marisa may also be in the above situation but know each other well and are probably of similar ages.

c) i) UNCLE NICK

    PLEASE DON'T GO OUT TILL THE PLUMBER CALLS (IF POSSIBLE). IF YOU'VE GOT A MINUTE, CAN YOU RING ME WITH THE BAD NEWS !!
          THANKS
          PAULA

  ii) Sergio

    I hope you've remembered — dinner is at 8 tonight. Come earlier than that if you want to.
          Geraldine

Exercise 7

Here are possible answers:

a) Gianni

    Electrician will bring fittings tonight so you can choose —
      See you this afternoon
          Lidia

b) Fred
    ~~Frank Woods~~ rang — bad news — job's off — gave it to a firm in Blackburn — he'll call back with details but you can ring him ~~before~~ 2.30.
          Jackie

c) Anna

    Hot Records called — your order is in — ask for <u>Lucy</u> if you go in tomorrow.
          Paulo

8 Advertisements

Exercise 1

a) There are many possibilities. Here is one example for each advertisement:
  ii) Lost. Sunglasses with white frame in green glasses case. Westside Shopping Centre. Sat. morning. Reward. Contact Sheri, 92 5487.
  ii) Man in early 50's, healthy, energetic, quite good-looking, interested in travel, would like to meet sincere, kind woman, 40–55 years old. Write to Box B12, The Courier, 404 South Rd.
  iii) Young woman, friendly, non-smoker, wants share accommodation in southern suburbs, preferably a house. Own furniture. Ring after 6p.m., 83 4549.

Exercise 3

b) Here are some possibilities:
  i) Capable, reliable, loving mother of two will mind child, from 2 months to 4 years old, in my home. Ph. 333 8720.
  ii) Odd jobs. Gardening, cleaning, rubbish removal, window cleaning. Just about anything! All those jobs you've been meaning to do for ages. Reasonable rates. Ring Lee. 929 4761.
  iii) Man, 35, non-smoker, wants to share flat/house near train line. Have some furniture. References available. Ring Andy 518745 or 287654.

9 Personal letters

Exercise 1

a) to thank
b) to express sadness on occasion of death
c) to make arrangements
d) to make contact or introduce oneself
e) to congratulate and express happiness on occasion of birth

Exercise 2

Here is one possible way to punctuate:

Perhaps Gail has told you about the new man in my life —
Paul Schleger. Sometimes I can't quite believe that there is
really someone in the world like him! Of course the problem is
that he's in Sydney, maybe moving back to Brisbane, while
I'm in Brisbane now, but moving to Perth. Why is love always
so difficult?

Exercise 3

a) i) C
   ii) E
   iii) D
   iv) A
   v) B

Exercise 4

a) *. . . I've taken months to reply — SORRY! It was great to hear from you at Christmas . . .*
   Glad to hear you've got some part-time work . . .
   What great news! You may be back here . . .
   Pleased to hear that Katy is . . .
   P.S. Thanks for those newspaper clippings — they were <u>very</u> interesting.
   P.P.S. You mentioned Tim Payne — what a surprise him leaving like that . . .

b)

> Dear Sarah,
>
> Thanks for your letter and for the terrific photos. You all look very sun-tanned and healthy! Glad you like the jumper, but I'm afraid your friends will have to knit their own — I'm too busy at present — sorry! You must be pleased to be finished that work — why don't you get yourself organized and do that word-processing course you've always wanted to do? Had a good laugh about you at political meetings — is this the same Sarah I know? Tell Bruce I want a judo exhibition on the January weekend — in his "pyjamas" of course!
>
> Well, let me tell you my news

10 Formal letters

Exercise 1

```
                                    (your address)

                                    (date)
Ms R. Douglas
Supervisor
H.H.D. Insurance
Hilton House
300 Pitt St
Sydney 2000

Dear Ms Douglas,
             I refer to your letter (JC:RD), dated 6th January 1988.
I wish to advise you that I have decided to cancel my Household
Contents Insurance policy. I would be grateful if you would
acknowledge receipt of my letter.
             Yours sincerely,
             (your signature)
             (your name)
```

Exercise 2

a) i) G   ii) E   iii) H   iv) F

b) Here are some possible opening sentences:

LETTER I

I am writing to enquire about child care facilities.
I would like some information on child care facilities.

LETTER J

I am writing in reply to your letter dated 4/3/88.
I received your letter dated 4/3/88.

Exercise 3

a) 11   b) 6   c) 2   d) 13   e) 12   f) 5   g) 1   h) 8   i) 3
j) 15   k) 14   l) 4   m) 7   n) 9   o) 10

Exercise 4

Dear Mr Anderson,
    I am writing to give you one month's notice of my intention to vacate the flat
at 1/35 Barker Rd, Malvern. The increase in the rent means that I can no longer
afford to live here. (iii) So should you have any flats available nearby that are
less expensive, I would be grateful if you would contact me. (i) In the meantime,
I have no objection to you showing people through the flat. (ii).
    Thanking you for your assistance.
    Yours sincerely,

Exercise 5

viii)
vii)
iv)
i)
vi)
v)
iii)
ii)

Exercise 6

i) and   ii) therefore   iii) however   iv) so

Exercise 7

Here are some possible ways to complete the formal notes:

i) Dear Mrs Deloso,

   I am sorry that I was unable to come for my appointment on Monday. Could I possibly make another appointment for next Monday at the same time?

ii) Dear Mr Nyland,

   Connie was absent from school for the last five days with the flu. I have enclosed a copy of the doctor's certificate.

iii) Dear Miss Phillips,

   Miguel was not at school this morning as he had an appointment at the dentist. He will be absent again next Tuesday morning as he has another appointment then.

11   Job applications

Exercise 1

Dear Sir/Madam,
   I am particularly interested in applying for the part-time position of gardener, advertised in the "Daily Planet" on March 14th.
   I am a keen horticulturist and am at present in the final year of a 3 year part-time course at Rosebank Technical College. I am specializing in the area of Australian native plants.

The position you offer would, therefore, be ideal for me. It would allow me to continue my studies and to work in an area where I can apply my specialist knowledge.

I have attached a résumé outlining my qualifications and experience.

Please contact me any time to arrange for an interview.

Yours sincerely,

Exercise 2

Here is one possible way to complete the letter:

Dear *Sir/Madam* ,

    I am writing to apply *for the position of Sales/Store person advertised in the "Morning Star" on 31st March.*

    I have worked as *a store person in a clothing warehouse for the past two years, and while at school I had a part-time job as a sales assistant in a news agency. I have a driver's licence and I speak Italian fluently.*

    I am *a reliable and enthusiastic worker* and I consider myself a most suitable applicant for the job.

    I have enclosed *a copy of my résumé and two references.*

    Please contact me *at any time, should you wish to arrange an interview.*

    Yours sincerely,

Exercise 6

i) employment
ii) interested
iii) experience
iv) recently
v) opportunity
vi) excellent
vii) available
viii) immediately
ix) necessary
x) résumé
xi) references
xii) vacancy
xiii) pleased

12 Letters of protest or complaint

Exercise 2

a) iii), vi), ii), v), i), vii), iv)
b) ii), i), vi), iii), v), vii), iv)

Exercise 3

a) ii)
b) iii) is best because the action to be taken is specified. However (ii) is also possible.
c) ii)
d) ii)
e) iii)

Exercise 4

i) realize/understand/accept/appreciate
ii) However
iii) protection
iv) unnecessary/ridiculous/excessive
v) extremely/very/unnecessarily/excessively
vi) (examples only)
   ○ and I can't hear my radio or television when it is on.
   ○ and I can hear clearly every word spoken on it.
vii) (examples only)
   ○ could something please be done
   ○ can you please do something
   ○ is it possible for something to be done
viii) (examples only)
   ○ consider the rights of the local residents when using the grounds.
   ○ take into account that people are trying to carry on with their daily lives nearby.
   ○ realize that football is not the only thing going on in the district, and restrict the disturbance it presently causes.
   ○ take my points into account and adjust their actions accordingly.
   You could also add a sentence to indicate some further action you might take:
   ○ If this letter does not get any response, I intend to take up the matter with the Noise Pollution Control Board / my local Member of Parliament / the Consumer Protection programme 'The Investigators'.

13 Letters of opinion

Exercise 1

Sir,

In reply to Mrs Childs' letter, (12/4/87), about working mothers, I would like to say that I totally disagree with her views.

Going out to work does not mean that your children are left alone without caring adults around them. Most working mothers are very concerned that their children are well looked after. I would also like to add that I am a working mother and that my children are healthy, happy, well-behaved and much loved.

If Mrs Childs thinks it is better for her to stay home with her children, that's fine. But she should allow other women to make up their own minds.

Exercise 2

b) Here are some possible answers:

i)	In the first place	v)	also
ii)	but	vi)	If
iii)	because	vii)	Therefore
iv)	Furthermore		

Exercise 3

iii), vi), i), iv), ii), v)

Acknowledgements

The authors and publishers are grateful to the authors, publishers and others who have given permission for the use of copyright material identified in the text. It has not been possible to identify the sources of all the material used and in such cases the publishers would welcome information from copyright owners.

Cover: story by Jim Sakkas by permission of 'The Times' Adult Migrant Education Services, Victoria; Rosemary Arias for 'No more Puff'; Werner Bartel Photography for the photograph of the Sydney Opera House.

Text: John Fairfax & Sons Ltd for the extracts from The Sun-Herald: about Don Lane on p. 8, the photograph on p. 8 by Ian Cugley, 'Christmas 100 years from now' on p. 17, 'Do you live like Krystle?' on p. 131; Mark David for the cartoon on p. 17; Transworld Feature Syndicate (UK) Ltd for the photograph on p. 131 by Yoram Kahana; The Canberra Times for the photograph on p. 27 by Martin Jones, the article 'Once robbed' on p. 76, the photograph on p. 125; The Manly Daily for the article 'Sun is an enemy' on p. 32; Australian Government Publishing Service for the leaflet on summer safety on pp. 37, 45, 135, 136, Commonwealth of Australia copyright, Department of Territories, 1986, and for the article 'Cocaine – the facts' on p. 91, National Campaign Against Drug Abuse, 1987; Dr Lyn Barrow for 'Aping the young' on p. 38 from The Sun-Herald; 'The Times' Adult Migrant Education Services, Victoria for the extracts on pp. 38 and 46; Eastern Suburbs Newspapers for the extracts from the Wentworth Courier: 'Postie' on p. 49, 'Travel diary' on p. 88, 'Ski' on p. 89, 'Cat lovers' on p. 130, 'Your news' on p. 131; The Canberra Chronicle for 'Are you a television addict?' on p. 131; T-Shirt Fair for the advertisement on p. 90; Women for a Nuclear Free Australia for the advertisement on p. 90; Cray Fish Industries Pty Ltd for the advertisement on p. 91; The NRMA magazine 'The Open Road' for the photographs on p. 114; The Daily Mirror for the article on p. 115; AAP Information Services for 'A report published' on p. 115, the text accompanying the drawing on p. 124, 'Panic in love nest' on p. 121; Neighbourhood Watch for the advertisement on p. 129; Barry Dwyer, Catholic Education Office, for the extract from his column in The Sun-Herald on p. 129; John Fairfax & Sons Ltd for extracts from the Sydney Morning Herald: 'What do you hate most' on p. 130 and 'It's service with a snarl' on p. 130.

Book design by Peter Ducker MSTD.
Cartoons by Shaun Williams (p. 26) and Dr Swami (pp. 115, 124).
Text artwork by Wenham Arts and Peter Ducker.